CREATORS OF MATHEMATICS
THE IRISH CONNECTION

The mathematicians illustrated on the front cover are (left to right): George Boole, William Thomson (Lord Kelvin), William Rowan Hamilton, George Francis Fitzgerald, George Gabriel Stokes, Patrick Brendan Kennedy and Andrew Young

Creators of Mathematics
The Irish Connection

edited by

Ken Houston

University College Dublin Press
Preas Choláiste Ollscoile Bhaile Átha Cliath

First published 2000 by University College Dublin Press
Newman House, 86 St Stephen's Green, Dublin 2, Ireland
www.ucdpress.ie

ISBN 1 900621 49 5

Cataloguing in Publication data available from the British Library

Typeset in 10.5/13 Photina by Elaine Shiels, Bantry, Co. Cork, Ireland
Printed in Ireland by ColourBooks, Dublin

Contents

Foreword

IRELAND HAS A DISTINGUISHED record of mathematical creativity. But this is not as widely known or as generally recognised as one might expect. Outside Ireland, although the major figures and their achievements are familiar, they tend to be grouped with other English-speaking mathematicians and the Irish association is often overlooked. The lack of awareness here in Ireland is less excusable; it is associated with a general neglect of history of science, particularly in our universities. Although there are signs of increasing interest, and an expanding output of relevant publications, we have still a long way to go. Within the Royal Irish Academy the National Committee for the History and Philosophy of Science has provided an important focus for individual scholars interested in the field. The Royal Dublin Society has also provided support and encouragement. Some good work has been done in Queen's University, Belfast. But we need a more serious engagement in research and teaching in the history and philosophy of science within our universities and must hope that we shall not have to wait too long to see this come about.

This book will undoubtedly help to raise the level of awareness of mathematical activity in Ireland, particularly during the nineteenth century. Some very well known and famous mathematicians are presented; others, much less well known, also appear. The emphasis in the individual entries is biographical. While they attempt to give the flavour of the subject's scientific work they generally avoid technical aspects and so, although holding a special fascination for those with an interest in mathematics, they should be accessible and interesting to a wide general readership.

The proposal to produce this book came from the National Committee for Mathematics of the Royal Irish Academy. The Academy has long been a focus for mathematical activity in Ireland – this was particularly the case through the nineteenth century – and so it is especially appropriate that it should be associated with this project. I congratulate the National Committee on its initiative. Special tribute is due to Professor Ken Houston who was chairman of the Committee from 1996 to 1999 and who undertook the task of editing the volume. I had the opportunity as a contributing author to appreciate the quiet efficiency with which he carried out that task. Our gratitude is also due to the University College Dublin Press, which readily accepted the invitation to publish the book, and to its Executive Editor, Barbara Mennell.

T.D. Spearman
President
Royal Irish Academy

List of Illustrations

Every effort has been made to trace the original copyright holders of illustrations, but if any have been overlooked, the publishers would be glad to make the necessary arrangements at the earliest opportunity.

Introduction

Ken Houston
University of Ulster, Jordanstown

T HIS BOOK IS A COLLECTION of biographies of some 'mathematicians with Irish connections' and it is written by practising, present day 'mathematicians with Irish connections'. The criteria for inclusion in the book are that the subjects should be mathematicians of one type or another who were born in Ireland or who worked here for a reasonable length of time, and who are now dead. The subjects include pure mathematicians, applied mathematicians/physicists and statisticians who have severally made a significant contribution to the development of their subject, who enjoyed an international reputation for their work in their time and whose ideas are important to mathematics today. The list of subjects is not comprehensive and one could point to eminent people who are not included, not because we feel they are unworthy but simply because no one of those approached by the editor felt moved to volunteer to write the biography.

The essays are arranged in chronological order by year of birth of the subjects. Most were born in the nineteenth century, one in the sixteenth and four in the twentieth. Some of the names, such as Hamilton and Boole, will be well known, but the others have also made significant contributions to the development of mathematics and the education of young mathematicians in Ireland, and the whole of the island is included. Our first subject, Thomas Harriot, sailed the seven seas with Sir Walter Ralegh in Elizabethan times, and the most recently deceased of our subjects, Sir David Bates, died in 1994.

The book is for the educated layman and for students who are training to be professionals. The biographies are intended to give a brief overview of the work of each subject, in non-technical language as far as is possible, and a brief picture of the personal life of each. Often knowledge of the personal circumstances of a subject gives insight into why he worked as he did. (Sadly there are no female subjects in our collection. There is at least one possible candidate but no one volunteered to write her story.)

The idea for this book came from the National Committee for Mathematics of the Royal Irish Academy, which comprises representatives from all universities and some other tertiary institutions in Ireland. It is intended to be part of the Irish contribution to the celebration of World Mathematics Year 2000 – WMY2K, and, of course, to the new millennium (which does not really start until 1 January 2001!). It was my privilege to be Chairman of the National Committee for Mathematics from 1996 to 1999 and I am delighted to be editing this collection. It took a little longer than originally planned to bring the book to a final state, but as 1999 draws to a close, it has, finally, all come together. I am grateful to the National Committee and to the Academy for their support and to all those who volunteered to write one or more biographies of their heroes.

1

Thomas Harriot 1560–1621

P. C. Fenton
University of Otago

T HOMAS HARRIOT WAS ONE OF the most influential mathematicians of the northern Renaissance. In the latter part of his life, as an esteemed scholar-pensioner in the household of the Earl of Northumberland, he evokes the figure of Prospero before his exile from Milan,

> neglecting worldly ends, all dedicated
> To closeness, and the bettering of my mind.

In his prime he was 'Ralegh's man', friend and adviser to Sir Walter Ralegh, and a vital participant in his boisterous affairs. In word and deed he represents the main currents of that remarkable age to which he belonged. Harriot was not Irish by birth or adoption. His place in this volume is warranted by his extended residence at Molanna Abbey, near Youghal, Co. Cork, during the later decades of the sixteenth century.

On 9 April 1585 a fleet of seven ships sailed out of Portsmouth harbour, bound for the new-found land of Virginia. A reconnaissance expedition organised by Walter Ralegh had returned a year before from the east coast of America, and the news it brought of a rich and fertile land had attracted investment in this new colonising enterprise. Among the 600 settlers, soldiers and crew was a 25-year-old mathematician, Thomas Harriot. Nothing is known of his early life save that he was born in Oxford and graduated with a Bachelor of Arts degree from St Mary's

Thomas Harriot

Hall, Oxford, in 1580. For two years prior to the voyage he had been employed as tutor in mathematics and navigation in Ralegh's household. Ralegh's earlier attempt to cross the Atlantic in 1578, a failure due to inadequate navigation, had convinced him of his need of someone of Harriot's abilities if his ambitions in the New World were to be realised. Harriot had already instructed the commanders of the reconnaissance, and written a text on navigation, *Arcticon*, for the purpose. No copies of the book survive but other evidence suggests that it was superior to its rivals in accuracy and clarity.

Harriot's duties were to supervise navigation and, once arrived in Virginia, to chart the coasts and rivers, and conduct a survey of the land and its inhabitants. He assembled his materials into a thin tract entitled *A Briefe and True Report of the New Found Land of Virginia*, his only work published during his lifetime. The book is in three parts, dealing with merchantable commodities, native flora and fauna, and, perhaps the most interesting, the manners and customs of the Indians. The style is modern in its analytical detail, its method the new one of observation and discovery.

Harriot assisted in planning the next attempt at settlement in 1587, the so-called Lost Colony, the fate of which remains a mystery to this day. By 1589 – probably even from the date of his return from Virginia in 1587 – he was in that other of Ralegh's colonial conquests, Ireland. A census taken on 12 May of that year lists Harriot as resident at Molanna Abbey, Co. Cork. He assisted in a survey of Ralegh's estates near Lismore in 1589, maintaining an involvement in the work until at least 1598. The Abbey house was sold by Harriot in 1597 for £200.

Ralegh and Harriot were well known to the popular imagination as scoffers and dabblers in dark arts. Such reputations were dangerous to possess. When the dramatist Thomas Kyd was investigated for distributing 'diverse lewd and mutinous libels', his rooms were found to contain 'vile and heretical conceits denying the deity of Christ'. He claimed that the papers were Christopher Marlowe's: 'For more assurance that I was not of that vile opinion, . . . enquire of such as he [Marlowe] conversed withall, that is (as I am given to understand) with Harriot, Warner, Royden . . .'. Another charge against Marlowe referred directly to Harriot. 'He affirmeth that Moses was but a Juggler, and that one Harriot being Sir Walter Ralegh's man can do more than he.' Marlowe was arrested, but by 30 May he was dead, murdered on Deptford Strand.

Accusations of atheism arose again in 1594. A commission was established to investigate heretical opinions of 'Sir Walter Ralegh, Mr Carew Ralegh, . . . , and one Harriot of Sir Walter Ralegh's House'. The evidence was all hearsay. Harriot is said to have 'brought the godhead in question', and to have denied the resurrection of the body; he is 'suspected of atheism'. In the end the inquiry was disbanded and no charges laid.

What is to be made of these accusations against Harriot? In *A Briefe and True Report*, Harriot wrote of the religion of the Indians from what appears to be a Christian perspective. In a much later letter to his physician (1616) he wrote: 'I believe in God Almighty, I believe that medicine was ordained by Him; I trust the physician as his minister. My faith is sure, my hope is firm.' A step or two from atheism or even deism. The Renaissance outlook was informed by a variety of mystical – and, to some, heretical – traditions that coexisted with Christian orthodoxy, including Neoplatonism, Pythagorean number mysticism, hermetic magic and a Christian interpretation of the Cabala, the esoteric Jewish doctrine that spread throughout Europe after the expulsion of the Jews from Spain in 1492.

Prior to this Harriot had joined the household of Henry Percy, 9th Earl of Northumberland. Ralegh and Northumberland had struck a close and enduring friendship, and shared an interest in literature and alchemical experimentation. Presumably Harriot fulfilled a dual role, serving Ralegh or Northumberland as circumstance required. But the character of his presence in both houses gradually altered. From being a paid servant, he became a pensioner, free to pursue his own researches. From 1590 until the early 1600s he investigated problems in navigation and cartography, ballistics, the estimation of specific gravities, and optics.

Harriot's most significant contributions to navigation were made in connection with the so-called Mercator problem, of finding a convenient scale to be employed in plotting parallels of latitude on a plane map: how is this to be done so that, if a straight line is drawn between two points on the map – as a master would do to determine his course – the angle made with the parallels is the compass bearing to be held in steering a course between the points? Hitherto the accepted scale was linear and known to be faulty, especially at high latitudes. It is easy to check that the latitude A ought to be plotted a distance

$$\int_0^A \sec t \, dt = \log \tan \left(\tfrac{\pi}{4} + \tfrac{A}{2} \right)$$

along the vertical axis. Harriot's achievement was to arrive at this result without the use of calculus or logarithms. An aside to his analysis was the determination of the area and length of an equiangular spiral. In related work in 1603 Harriot discovered the formula for the area of a spherical triangle with given angles.

Throughout the sixteenth century the study of ballistics was hampered by Aristotelian analysis, according to which the elements earth, water, air and fire have natural places and tend to seek them. It was felt that a cannon ball would proceed first in a straight line while under the immediate influence of the explosion of gunpowder, would then execute a small circular motion, and subsequently fall almost vertically towards its natural place, the centre of the earth. Harriot's ballistics papers are fragmentary, and it appears that he never entirely freed himself from Aristotle, but by 1607 he had arrived (by a way which is not clear) at the correct conclusion, that the path of a projectile is parabolic.

In the late 1590s Harriot began a series of experiments on the refraction of light which led to his discovery of the sine law in 1603, anticipating Snell by almost 20 years. Later he turned his attention to the refractive indices of various substances for different colours, and wrote to Kepler of his intention to publish an account of colours and the rainbow.

In 1599 Harriot spent a concentrated period on alchemical experiments. A prim view is sometimes taken of this work as though it were unworthy of a true scientist. But its essential doctrines have counterparts in modern physics, and even its mystical aspect is not alien to the scientific spirit.

Harriot's algebraic manuscripts are characterised by a remarkable clarity, deriving in part from his notational innovations. Most of these have been superseded but his symbols < and > for inequality survive. He investigated algebraic equations up to the quintic, allowing both negative and complex roots with unprecedented confidence. In performing calculations in relation to the Mercator problem, he introduced the binomial coefficients C_p^n and examined their properties, allowing n to be positive or negative, even fractional. He experimented with binary enumeration, which, together with his 'atomistic pseudo-philosophy', as one of his contemporaries described his atomic view of matter, lends him a prophetic aspect.

None of this work was published during his lifetime, and his reluctance to do so contributed to his subsequent neglect. He wrote to Kepler in 1608 that 'our situation is such that I still may not philosophise freely;

we are still stuck in the mud'. As his interests inclined more and more to astronomy and the new cosmology, the risk of advertising his views only increased.

With the accession of James to the English throne, Ralegh was stripped of his place at court and eventually, in 1603, summoned to answer a charge of treason. He was condemned to death, although the sentence was later reduced to life imprisonment. How nearly this affected Harriot is revealed in the records of the trial. In his summing up, the Lord Chief Justice attacked certain 'very atheistical and profane precepts' attributed to Ralegh. 'If not yours you shall do very well to protest against them. If yours then renounce them and . . . let not Harriot nor any such Doctor persuade you there is no eternity'. After 1603 Harriot took up permanent residence with Northumberland at Syon House near Kew.

Northumberland's disenchantment with James grew, and in 1605 he retired to Syon to follow his scientific and literary interests. On the afternoon of 4 November 1605 he was visited at Syon by his cousin Thomas Percy, one of the conspirators in the Gunpowder Plot. After the events of the following day Northumberland was committed to the Tower, and Harriot was questioned and briefly imprisoned. A letter in which Harriot petitioned for his release has survived. 'All that know me', he wrote, 'can witness that I was always of honest conversation and life. I was never any busy meddler in matters of state. I was never ambitious for preferments. But contented with a private life for the love of learning that I might study freely.' He was back at Syon early in 1606.

The remainder of Harriot's life was passed in relative obscurity. His interests turned to astronomy, and he made notable observations with 'perspective trunks', as he called his telescopes. In 1607 he had observed by the naked eye what is known now as Halley's comet. In 1609 he made several moon maps, and from 1610 until 1613 was engaged in recording sunspots.

Meanwhile Ralegh, chafing against his confinement, had formulated plans for an expedition in search of El Dorado. He was freed to take command of a small fleet, on condition that, at pain of his life, he avoid interference with Spanish interests, which was practically impossible. He sailed in June 1617, and, after an engagement with a party of Spaniards, returned to England, and was condemned. Among Harriot's papers is a sheet of notes recording Ralegh's speech from the scaffold. The companion of Ralegh's triumphs was his companion still on the cold October morning at the end of his fall.

A cancerous tumour of the nostril, first noticed in 1613, began to affect Harriot's health. The circumstance that Harriot smoked tobacco, a legacy of his Virginia period, was not lost on his physician. He died on 2 July 1621. It is the least enviable of his many claims to priority that Harriot's may have been the first recorded death from cancer induced by tobacco smoke. He was buried in the church of St Christopher-le-Stocks, and in 1622 Northumberland had raised in the chancel a monument to 'that most learned Harriot of Syon on the river Thames, His birthplace and school Oxford He cultivated all knowledges And excelled in all. Mathematics, Philosophy, Science, Theology'. An idle jotting among Harriot's papers perhaps reveals something of his view of himself, and might serve as another, less reverential epitaph. The first line is a well-known proverb, the other apparently Harriot's own addition:

> A man of words and not of deeds is like a garden full of weeds.
> A man of deeds and not of words is like a privy full of turds.

Bibliography

Thomas Harriot, *A Briefe and True Report of the New Found Land of Virginia*, Dover reprint, 1972.

J. A. Lohne (1972) 'Thomas Harriot', *Dictionary of Scientific Biography*, VI, New York.

Muriel Rukeyser (1971) *The Traces of Thomas Hariot*, New York.

J. W. Shirley (ed.) (1974) *Thomas Harriot, Renaissance Scientist*, Oxford.

J. W. Shirley (1983) *Thomas Harriot, A Biography*, Oxford.

Sir William Rowan Hamilton was President of the Royal Irish Academy, 1837–46, and this portrait by an unknown artist hangs in the Academy.

2

William Rowan Hamilton 1805–65

T. D. Spearman
Trinity College, Dublin

WILLIAM ROWAN HAMILTON WAS BORN in Dublin, in his father's house in Dominick Street, in 1805. Both of his parents were Dubliners: his father Archibald, the son of an apothecary, had served his apprenticeship in an attorney's office and now conducted his own modest legal practice. Both father and grandfather were Freemen of the city of Dublin and his great-uncle Francis Hamilton had been an Alderman. William's mother Sarah came of a family called Hutton who owned a coach-building firm. For various reasons, William was sent off at the age of three to live under the tutelage of his uncle James, who ran the diocesan school at Trim in Co. Meath. He stayed there, apart from short vacation visits to his family, until he entered Trinity College some 15 years later. The Rev. James Hamilton was a classicist with some knowledge of oriental languages – he recognised his nephew's precocious talent and fed him an extraordinary diet of the classics, of Hebrew and of a wide range of oriental and modern languages.

William appears to have been quite happy at Trim. It was a quiet, pleasant town, historically interesting and relatively insulated from the poverty and hardship to be seen in much of the country. The school was small but had some tradition: the Duke of Wellington had attended it briefly some thirty years earlier, and the building in which it was housed had once belonged to Dean Swift. James was quite a taskmaster, albeit a kindly and supportive one, and his nephew responded positively.

Uncle James observed William's remarkable computational skill but he was not competent, and probably not inclined, to encourage his mathematical bent. He did, however, produce for him a copy of Bartholomew Lloyd's *Analytical Geometry*, which was to have a decisive effect. William was then sixteen, and his eyes were opened. He wrote 'Ill-omened gift! It was the commencement of my present course of mathematical reading, which has in so great a degree withdrawn my attention, I may say my affection, from the Classics.'

Hamilton entered Trinity College in 1823. He was particularly fortunate that, in the decade immediately preceding his entry, the teaching of mathematics within the College had been altered almost beyond recognition; the new methods from France and Germany were brought into the curriculum, the French texts were introduced and new textbooks were written in English expounding the recent continental work. The chief architect of this reform was Bartholomew Lloyd, who was Professor of Mathematics from 1813 to 1822, then Professor of Natural Philosophy until elected Provost in 1831. Although Bartholomew Lloyd was not himself a creative mathematician, he clearly appreciated the developments that had taken place within the subject and he had the administrative ability to introduce the necessary radical changes.

There is no indication that the discipline of regular examinations was harmful to him; the revised syllabus was reasonably stimulating, even to Hamilton, and he had every opportunity and encouragement to read outside the course. His tutor, Charles Boyton, was a widely read and intelligent man – a competent mathematician who, although he did not produce original work himself, could encourage and guide his brilliant student and appears generally to have been an excellent tutor.

Hamilton's earliest attempts at original work were in geometry. His studies of the work of the French geometer Monge on families of surfaces and their normals suggested a new approach to optics based on systems of rays, treated mathematically as rectilinear congruences. Within a year of entering College he had submitted his first paper, describing this work, to the Royal Irish Academy. It was referred back with the recommendation that he should develop his ideas further before resubmitting. Hamilton did that, adding substantially to what he had already written, and in 1827 his first famous paper, *Theory of Systems of Rays*, was read before the Academy. His achievement did not pass unrecognised. Brinkley, the Andrews Professor of Astronomy, had just been appointed to the bishopric of Cloyne and the youthful Hamilton, before he had actually graduated, was elected to the Andrews Chair. This appointment was remarkable, as the new incumbent had almost no practical experience in astronomical observation and the potential field for the job included some able men of established reputation. Hamilton's appointment to this post, which since 1792 had carried the title of Astronomer Royal of Ireland, was, of course, profoundly significant in the extent to which it shaped his subsequent career.

Fortunately the new Astronomer Royal did not feel constrained to devote himself unduly to astronomy, although he continued for some time with his important and highly original work in optics. He was, however, conscious of his responsibility to carry out observations and measurements, and to process and analyse these. Immediately following his appointment he went to stay with Brinkley at Cloyne, receiving valuable advice and guidance; he then accepted the invitation of Thomas Romney Robinson to spend some time with him at the Armagh Observatory to gain practical experience. This helped him to assume responsibility for the round of routine observations which were made with the help of his assistant and his own two sisters who lived with him in the Observatory. His position, with a house at Dunsink (a few miles out of Dublin) and a secure, if not overgenerous, salary was less demanding than a Tutorial Fellowship which he would otherwise normally have held.

The field of optics, to which Hamilton was still devoting his main efforts, had recently moved back into the centre of the scientific stage. This followed the discovery of the phenomenon of interference by Thomas Young, and subsequently the publication of two highly significant memoirs by Augustin Jean Fresnel in the early 1820s. For over a century the conflict between the wave and corpuscular theories of light had remained unresolved. Sir Isaac Newton had been led to reject the wave theory because the type of wave which would be required was transverse rather than longitudinal and he could not conceive of a mechanism whereby transverse light waves could propagate. He concluded that light must be corpuscular in nature. When Young demonstrated the phenomenon of interference for light this pointed strongly towards a wave interpretation, as interference effects were already familiar features of wave systems – in sound, for example, or in water waves.

Among the various observed phenomena which any theory of light would have to encompass was that known as double refraction. This remarkable phenomenon had been discovered in 1669 by Bartholomeus. Certain crystals – in particular that known as Iceland spar – gave a double image. This meant that a single ray of light entering the crystal produced two refracted rays, and the phenomenon was known as double refraction.

Christiaan Huygens, as early as 1690, had invented an elegant and clever procedure for describing wave propagation, which could also allow for the simpler cases of double refraction. But the more complicated phenomenon in so-called biaxial crystals could not be described by this method. Fresnel's remarkable achievement was to devise a model for the propagation of transverse light waves in crystals, which led to Huygens's construction where that was applicable but which could also describe the more complicated phenomena involving biaxial crystals. Fresnel's method was mathematically quite involved – it led to wave surfaces which were geometrically rather complicated and whose properties were by no means immediately obvious from their equations.

Hamilton, of course, knew and was deeply interested in Fresnel's results. By one of these strokes of either luck or genius, probably somewhere between the two, Hamilton noticed a remarkable feature of the wave-surface which meant that for a particular direction of the incident ray on a biaxial crystal, instead of double refraction there should be a quite new effect: instead of a double image, of each incident ray producing two refracted rays, in this special case each incident ray should give rise to a complete cone of refracted rays. Hamilton immediately described his discovery to his Trinity colleague Humphrey Lloyd and suggested that he should perform the experiment to see if this new and quite unexpected phenomenon did in fact occur. If it did it would appear to be a striking corroboration of the Fresnel theory and by implication of the wave theory of light. Humphrey, who was the son of Bartholomew Lloyd, had just been appointed to the Chair of Natural Philosophy in Trinity. Although his background and training were in mathematics, he had become interested in experiment and it was as an experimental physicist working in optics and in geomagnetism that he was to achieve distinction. The experiment proposed by Hamilton was not an easy one, the effect was easily obscured and the quality of the crystals available to Lloyd was relatively poor, so the positive outcome was a tribute to Lloyd's consider-able skill, as well as his patience and persistence.

The observation of conical refraction was generally seen as a powerful confirmation of the wave theory – the evidence for which was by now hard to reject, despite the reservations about the hypotheses underlying Fresnel's theory and the problems posed by the newly observed absorption phenomena. This was a remarkable discovery and a triumph for Hamilton in particular. It was one of the classic vindications of the scientific method. Fresnel's theory had been constructed to accommodate known experimental results; from it, following quite elaborate mathematical argument, a new prediction was extracted, a prediction which could not have been anticipated and in fact must have seemed rather improbable. Recognition followed swiftly. At the 1834 meeting of the British Association in Edinburgh, Lloyd was invited to give the main review talk in Physical Optics and in 1836 he was elected to the Royal Society. In 1835, the year following the Edinburgh meeting at which Lloyd presented his report, the British Association met in Dublin and on this occasion Hamilton, who acted as local secretary and organiser of the meeting, now at the age of thirty a famous man, was knighted by the Lord Lieutenant.

Hamilton's interest now moved from optics to dynamics. In fact this did not represent a total change of direction, for his approach to dynamics, described in his two *Essays on a General Method in Dynamics*, closely paralleled his approach to optics. This parallelism between optics and dynamics emphasised by Hamilton was to become particularly significant in the twentieth century with the introduction of wave mechanics. Today many would regard Hamilton's dynamics as his most important work, although at the time it was published it did not attract a great deal of interest. It was really only in the present century that the power and generality of the Hamiltonian methods came to be appreciated. Perhaps the most important influence was that on Erwin Schrödinger who received a thorough grounding in Hamiltonian dynamics from his professor, Hasenöhrl, who, in turn, was a student of Sommerfeld. Schrödinger gave the Hamiltonian formulation a central role in his construction of quantum mechanics. Today every physicist is familiar with the Hamiltonian function, which is the typical starting-point for almost any type of dynamical calculation.

From the mid-1830s until his death in 1865, Hamilton's preoccupation was with algebraic questions, the culminating achievement – which in his own mind outweighed all his other work – being the discovery of quaternions in 1843. Hamilton believed that quaternions would provide a valuable key for the understanding of the physical world. This belief has not been vindicated – in fact quaternions have made little direct contribution to the development of physics. The profound and lasting influence of Hamilton's work in algebra, which began with his description of complex numbers as number pairs and was followed by the discovery of quaternions and the recognition of their non-commutativity, was the

Brougham Bridge, Dublin. A plaque marks the spot where Sir William Rowan Hamilton carved the formula for quaternion multiplication on 16 October 1843.

stimulus which it gave to the development of algebra as an abstract axiomatic discipline. There is some irony in this. Hamilton was led towards quaternions by a deep metaphysical motivation based particularly on his reading of Kant. First pointed in that direction by his friend Coleridge, Hamilton had grappled with the German original of the *Critique of Pure Reason*. Like his literary friends, he had a natural sympathy for the idealism which Kant propounded. But he also found in the *Critique* technical answers to the questions which he regarded as fundamental to his mathematics. Hamilton wanted an intuitive interpretation for the objects of mathematics. He could not accept a mathematics in which the basic elements were merely symbols. Following Kant, he gave meaning to the number system through the intuition of pure time. Starting with this intuition, which he regarded as fundamental, he constructed the real numbers, then the complex numbers as pairs of real numbers, and then quaternions. Hamilton's outlook parallels that of Brouwer and the Intuitionists of the twentieth century, whose constructive approach to mathematics contrasts with the emphasis on consistency alone which marks the more widely held formalist viewpoint. The interesting historical fact is that it was the intuitionist approach of Hamilton which led to the radical idea of a non-commutative algebra. The formalist outlook of his Cambridge contemporaries could in principle permit non-commutativity without any difficulty, but until Hamilton constructed the algebra of quaternions the old laws, derived from the real number system, remained sacrosanct.

Hamilton's own account of his discovery of quaternions, the resolution of the problem which had thwarted and frustrated him for over a decade, is well known. It is an authentic and compelling description of the moment of discovery. The date was the sixteenth of October in 1843. He was walking from Dunsink into town to attend a meeting in the Academy.

> I then and there felt the galvanic circuit of thought close; and the sparks which fell from it were the fundamental equations between i, j, k; . . . I felt a problem to have been at that moment solved – an intellectual want relieved – which had haunted me for at least fifteen years before.

Hamilton straight away recorded these equations, which give the multiplication law for his so-called quaternions, in his pocket book.

> Nor could I resist the impulse – unphilosophical as it may have been – to cut with a knife on a stone of Brougham Bridge, as we passed it, the fundamental formula.

Hamilton's personal life was not the brilliant success of his academic and professional career. The unrequited love for Catherine Disney, thwarted by her enforced and unhappy marriage to the Rev. William Barlow, their last meeting as she lay dying, when Hamilton on his knees presented her with his book *Lectures on Quaternions*; his own unsuitable and lonely marriage with the semi-invalid Helen Bayly and the lack of an orderly domestic regime owing to his wife's frequent illness and absence from home; periodic financial anxieties and an occasional drink problem; all this is the stuff of which romantic novels are made. But he had many close friends in whom he could confide and with whom he maintained a lively correspondence. Apart from his academic colleagues these included, for example, the Dunravens, whose son Lord Adare had been his pupil and lived for a time with him in Dunsink, and the de Veres who lived in Curragh Chase, set in what has been described as one of the most remote and romantic settings conceivable. Tennyson came to Curragh Chase to visit his and Hamilton's friend Aubrey de Vere. On one occasion as a young man Hamilton had come down from Dublin apparently determined to propose marriage to Ellen de Vere, but allowed himself to be too easily discouraged. His faint heart in love was in contrast with his assurance and resolution in science. Maria Edgeworth, the novelist, and her family were also close friends. Another friend was Lady Wilde, or Speranza as she was known, who invited him to be godfather to her son Oscar; her little pagan, she called him, which may have been what prompted Hamilton, for whom the responsibility of a godparent would not have been taken lightly, to decline.

Hamilton was strongly influenced by the Romantic movement and this accorded with his natural temperament. Wordsworth, whom he visited on several occasions and who came to stay in Dunsink, was a much admired friend. He also knew Coleridge: it was probably Coleridge who introduced him to the philosophy of Kant. Hamilton's science, as we have seen, was much influenced by his philosophical views. At first these were strongly Berkleian, not surprising in Trinity at the time; later, when he discovered Kant he responded enthusiastically and the Kantian view of algebra as the science of pure time was undoubtedly a key motivating influence in his algebraic work.

Poetry was a continuing passion for him although, guided gently by Wordsworth, he had come to accept that his own vocation was as a mathematician and not as a poet. But he still wrote verse prolifically, apparently finding it easier to express his deeper sentiments in this way, particularly in sonnet form. And he saw mathematics as poetic in nature and judged the work of his contemporaries in poetical terms. Among the French mathematicians Fourier and Lagrange commanded his particular respect. He wrote:

> Fourier was a true poet in Mathematics, and in the applications of mathematical science to nature (especially to the theory of heat). So was (though not Laplace) Lagrange, to whose memory I consider as having inscribed those essays on a general method in dynamics.

Politically, Hamilton might be described as a moderate conservative. He was a committed member of the Anglican Church of Ireland and a firm supporter of the established order.

Hamilton was President of the Royal Irish Academy from 1837 until 1846. He was deeply committed to the Academy, attached considerable significance to his responsibilities as president and worked assiduously to promote the Academy's interests. As would be expected, he received many honours. His knighthood was conferred in 1835. The previous year he had been awarded the Cunningham Medal of the Academy and the Royal Medal of the Royal Society, both of these in recognition of his work in optics and in particular the discovery of conical refraction. He was an honorary member of many learned societies, but perhaps the best indication of his international standing is that when the National Academy of Sciences was founded in the United States and a choice was made of distinguished foreign scientists to be elected Foreign Associates, Hamilton's name was first on the list.

William Rowan Hamilton died in 1865. The President of the Royal Irish Academy at that time was Charles Graves and it fell to him to make an obituary address to the Academy at its Stated Meeting. Charles Graves was a Fellow of Trinity College and Professor of Mathematics. He was one of Hamilton's close and loyal friends. He should have the last word:

> Hamilton was gifted with a rare combination of those qualities which are essential instruments of discovery. He had that fine perception of analogy by which the investigator is guided in his passage from the known to the unknown. This is an instrument by which many important mathematical discoveries have been effected. But he seems, also, to have possessed a higher power of divination – an intuitive perception that new truths lay in a particular direction, and that patient and systematic search, carried on within definite limits, must certainly be rewarded by the discovery of a path leading into regions hitherto unexplored. Something like this was

the unshaken assurance which led Columbus to turn his back upon Europe, to launch upon the broad Atlantic, and seek a New World in the far-off West.

Note

In writing this chapter I have drawn significantly on a Discourse which I gave at the Royal Irish Academy, the full text of which is published in *Proceedings of the Royal Irish Academy*, **95a**, Supplement, 1995, pp. 1–12.

3

Robert Murphy 1806–43

Leo Creedon
University of Alberta

R OBERT MURPHY WAS BORN in 1806 in the town of Mallow, Co. Cork. He grew up on Beecher Street, the sixth of nine children of John and Margaret Murphy. John Murphy was a shoemaker, and also served as parish clerk. This ensured a modest income, and showed that he had at least some formal education. Things took a turn for the worse, however, when John died in January 1814, leaving his family in destitution. Robert was seven at this time, and, rarely blessed with good fortune, he suffered another calamity three years later when he was run over by a cart while playing in the street outside his house. His thighbone was fractured and Robert was confined to bed for a year and spent a further six months of recovery on his feet.

Some good came of this, however, as it was during this time of enforced leisure that Robert discovered that he had a talent for mathematics. Books were hard to come by, but his mother gave him a Cork almanac in which he found problems on tides, navigation, trigonometry and astronomy. It had been assumed that Robert would be a shoemaker himself when he came of age, but given his obvious mathematical ability, he was provided with Euclid's Geometry and an algebra text. In 1819, a man named Mulcahy (whose son was later to become a Professor of Mathematics at Queen's College, Galway) was a teacher in Cork. Mulcahy posed mathematical problems in a local newspaper, and began to receive unusual solutions from an anonymous reader in Mallow. Mulcahy travelled to Mallow and was astonished to discover that his correspondent was a thirteen-year-old child. Mulcahy spoke to Robert's family, and seeing their poverty, he elicited help from their neighbour Mr Croker and from Mr Hopley, the principal of the local school. Robert entered Hopley's school under the instruction of a Mr Armstrong, with his fees and books paid for by the principal.

In 1823, Mulcahy, Croker and Hopley sponsored Murphy's application to Trinity College, Dublin, submitting some of his original work as evidence of his talents. Despite the credentials of his sponsors, his application was doomed by the brevity of his formal education and the incomprehensibility of his work. The Queen's Colleges of Cork, Galway, and Belfast had not yet been established, so young Murphy would have to look further afield to continue his education. At the time, Cambridge was the centre of the English-speaking mathematical world (in those days this was not as great a claim as it sounds), and must have seemed the ideal, if unrealistic, destination for Murphy.

In 1824, a young priest named John Mackey, a student at Maynooth College and originally from Cashel, published a pamphlet in which he purported to have shown a method of constructing the cube root of 2, using only a straight edge and compass. This appeared to be a solution of an ancient problem which had defied assault by the greatest mathematical minds of modern times. Murphy had studied such problems, and suspected that they had no solution (we now know that Murphy was correct in his suspicions). Murphy spotted an error in Fr Mackey's work and published a pamphlet with the impressive title 'Refutation of a Pamphlet written by the Rev. John Mackey, RCP, entitled "A method of making a cube double of a cube, founded on the principles of elementary geometry", wherein his principles are proved erroneous, and the required solution not yet obtained'. While it was a remarkable work for a poorly educated teenager it did not ensure financial security for the maturing young mathematician.

Murphy had a second chance at admission to a university when he met a Mr McCarthy, a junior fellow at Gonville and Caius College, Cambridge. McCarthy was back in Cork on vacation, and hearing of Murphy he brought some of his work back to Caius with him and presented it to Professor Robert Woodhouse. Incidentally, Woodhouse himself was a hugely influential figure in the history of mathematics, not so much for his own work, but for the reforms he introduced into British mathematics from the continent. These reforms ended England's insular mathematical tradition and addiction to defending the honour of Isaac Newton, including his cumbersome notation for derivatives. Without Woodhouse there might have been no Cambridge reformers (George Peacock, John Herschel and Charles Babbage), much less continental mathematical influence and none of the flowering of abstract algebra that occurred in England and Ireland in the second half of the nineteenth century, which Murphy also helped commence. In any case, Professor Woodhouse initially had the same response to Murphy's application as his Trinity colleagues, but upon a second reading he saw the potential of Murphy's work. Woodhouse wrote to McCarthy saying that Murphy would be admitted to Caius on a reduced fee of £60, and if his friends could raise this amount, their charity would not be called upon again. Murphy's patrons rose to the task, and in October 1825, Murphy set out to begin studies at the very centre of British mathematics.

Murphy acquitted himself admirably as an academic, receiving many awards and honours. However, he still found himself in relative poverty at Cambridge. Murphy graduated in 1828 and was appointed to the Perse Fellowship, to a position as junior dean (in charge of discipline and reading prayers) and also worked as librarian, Greek lecturer and Hebrew lecturer to help supplement his still modest income.

All of Murphy's greatest mathematical works appear in the eight short years from 1830 to 1837. This was the brief interval between his toil as an undergraduate and the final decline of his health and finances.

In 1830 Murphy presented a paper on integrals, and was commissioned to write a textbook on electricity for the students at Cambridge. This he completed in 1833, and he went on to publish three important papers on integral equations. He also wrote several papers on the roots of polynomials, and an advanced textbook on algebraic equations which appeared in 1839.

In 1836 Murphy published a paper called 'First memoir on the theory of analytical operations'. Despite this title, no later memoirs were to appear on this subject, probably owing to Murphy's deteriorating personal circumstances. This paper broke new ground in analysis and algebra. Analytically, it provided the theoretical background for a great deal of work in differential equations, including George Boole's 1844 paper 'On a general method of analysis' for which Boole won the first Royal Medal ever awarded by the Royal Society of London for a work in pure mathematics. Ironically, this paper helped Boole gain a position as the first professor of mathematics at the newly founded Queen's College, Cork. In contrast, Murphy's paper did not help to rescue him from his decline and early death in London.

It is worth mentioning something of the mathematical content of Murphy's paper on the theory of linear operations. Let $f(x)$ be a function of x. We consider $f(x)$ as the *Subject*, and perform an *Operation* on it to get the *Result*. For example, if Δ represents taking a finite difference, then $\Delta(f(x)) = f(x + h) - f(x)$. Murphy considers only linear operators, i.e. functions θ such that $\theta(f(x) + g(x)) = \theta f(x) + \theta g(x)$ and $\theta k f(x) = k\theta f(x)$, where k is a real number. To a modern analyst these are linear operators, and to an algebraist they are R–module homomorphisms. Murphy now makes an important abstraction, and considers these operators as the objects of interest, irrespective of the functions they operate upon. Two of these operators are equal if, given any subject, they return the same result. So we may speak of equality of operations. We may add operations α and β by defining $(\alpha + \beta)f(x) = \alpha f(x) + \beta f(x)$. We may multiply operations by defining $\alpha\beta f(x) = \alpha(\beta f(x))$. Thus, α^n means the operation you get when you perform α n consecutive times on a subject.

So Murphy develops an arithmetic of operations, but the interesting aspect of all of this is the fact that two operations α and β need not be commutative. In other words the operation $\alpha\beta$ need not equal $\beta\alpha$. Murphy refers to two commuting operations as relatively free, and to non-commuting operations as relatively fixed. This leads to some interesting discoveries in elementary abstract algebra. For example, Murphy states and proves the binomial theorem for two non-commuting variables (and also the more familiar version for commuting variables). He defines the exponential e^α of an operation α. Murphy notes that the sum or product of two operations is again an operation, so the astute algebraist can now relax in the knowledge that Murphy has defined a non-commutative ring. We should note that all of this was published eight years before W.R. Hamilton's 1844 paper 'On quaternions'. The multiplicative identity of this ring is the operation 1, meaning 'multiply the subject by one'.

Murphy next explores the existence of the multiplicative inverse of operations. As was widely known, differentiation is a linear operator, and integration (or, more accurately, anti-differentiation) is the obvious candidate for the inverse operation to differentiation. However, since, for example, $\frac{d}{dx}(x + 2) = 1$, and $\int 1 dx = x + C$, where C is some arbitrary constant, Murphy noticed that speaking of the inverse of an operation would not be as straightforward as the idea of the reciprocal of a real number.

Modern algebraists have overcome this difficulty by considering the kernel of a homomorphism. It was Murphy, I believe, who first came up with this idea, when he wrote of 'the *appendage* of an operation'. If α is the operation and $f(x)$ is the subject under consideration, let $\alpha f(x) = g(x)$ be the result. The kernel (appendage) of α is defined to be the set of all subjects P such that $\alpha P = 0$. Then Murphy defines the inverse $\alpha^{-1}g(x) = f(x) + P$.

When inverses of two operations do exist (i.e. when the kernels are zero), Murphy showed that to invert the product of two operations 'we must invert the *order* as well as the nature of the component operations'. That is to say, $(\alpha\beta)^{-1} = \beta^{-1}\alpha^{-1}$. He also noted that $(\alpha^n)^{-1} = \alpha^{-n}$. Murphy goes on to consider the conjugates $\alpha^{-1}\beta\alpha$ and Lie brackets $(\alpha\beta - \beta\alpha)$ of operations. He then applies his ideas to prove some classical and new results in ordinary and partial differential equations. This work was the forerunner of a great deal of activity in abstract algebra and differential equations.

While from the years 1830 to 1836 Murphy's mathematical career seemed to be proceeding very well, his private life was not progressing so healthily. During these years he recorded hundreds of bets in the wagers book of Gonville and Caius College. Many of these bets were with William Haughton Stokes, elder brother of George Gabriel Stokes. Murphy's dissipated habits seem to have got the better of him, and in December 1832 he lost his job as dean. Murphy managed to repay his debt to his patron Mr Hopley (in fact he sent the money to his widow), but he had gone deeply into debt while in Cambridge. Murphy certainly had a gambling problem, and was perhaps an alcoholic. Eventually, in 1836, he was forced to leave Cambridge under a cloud, with bills throughout the town left unpaid, and his fellowship sequestered to repay his debts. James Cockle wrote of 'the great genius of the lamented analyst', while Augustus DeMorgan explained that Murphy, whose 'career, though great in mathematics, fell short in conduct and discretion. He wanted all but mathematical education in early youth', and again wrote that 'There is much excuse for a very young man, brought up in penury and pushed by the force of early talent into a situation in which ample command of money is accompanied by even more than proportionate exposure to temptation'. Murphy, from a working-class Irish background, probably still limping from his childhood accident, suddenly found himself relocated into a world of wealth, pomp and social status. It should also be noted that Murphy's father had died when Robert was only seven, and he had been raised solely by his mother. Her death in August 1832 must have come as a severe blow to him.

In any case, the discipline of his undergraduate years was relaxed, and Murphy, his paradise lost, may have returned to Ireland for a time, until eventually, with the help of his friend Augustus DeMorgan, he managed to find employment as examiner in mathematics and natural philosophy at the University of London. While living in London, Caius awarded him a more valuable fellowship, but this too was confiscated to repay his Cambridge debts, leaving him relying on the meagre fees he charged for the private tutorials he was giving. As celibacy was one of the requirements of holding a Cambridge fellowship, Murphy never married, since he could not have supported even himself without it. He completed an algebra textbook in 1839, but even before this he was complaining of poor health and he developed a disease of the lungs, probably tuberculosis. This caused him to lose his students, making his financial situation even worse. Murphy's early death left much of his work uncompleted, leaving only suggestions of the greatness he might otherwise have achieved. Robert Murphy died in London on 12 March 1843 at the age of thirty-seven.

4

George Boole 1815–64

Desmond MacHale

University College Cork

GEORGE BOOLE, MATHEMATICIAN, LOGICIAN AND one of the fathers of the modern computer, was born in the City of Lincoln in the East of England in 1815. His father, John Boole, was an impecunious shoemaker. He was more interested in the making of telescopes and other optical instruments with which to view the stars and other natural phenomena than he was in running a successful business. The result was that George had to leave school at the age of around fourteen and take a job as an assistant teacher to support his parents, his two brothers, and his sister. Thus George Boole received no formal second-level or third-level education and was largely self-taught throughout his life. However, he immersed himself in study, borrowing and devouring every book he could lay his hands on. Initially he was interested in languages, and was fluent in classical Latin and Greek by the astonishingly early age of ten; later he acquired French, Italian and German, all without the aid of a tutor.

From his father he inherited a love of science, and together they made, starting from scratch, many instruments such as beam balances, tele-scopes, and some say even a primitive calculator. An interest in astronomy naturally followed, and the young George was drawn into the worlds of physics, applied mathematics, and finally mathematics. His knowledge of continental languages meant that by the age of eighteen he was reading in their original versions the works of the great masters Lagrange and

Laplace at a time when most other British mathematicians were still slavishly following Isaac Newton.

By now Boole had opened his own day and boarding school in Lincoln which he ran with the help of his family. In his spare time he did original research in mathematics which was good enough to be published in the *Cambridge Journal of Mathematics*. Boole would have loved to become a student at the University of Cambridge and mix with all the great mathematicians there such as Gregory, Cayley, Kelvin and others, but his poor family circumstances would not allow it.

Boole's first published research papers were in the areas of the differential and integral calculus and in particular he gave ingenious new methods for the evaluation of integrals. In 1841 he actually invented a whole new branch of mathematics – Invariant Theory, which was later to be very important when Einstein was laying the foundations of the Theory of Relativity at the turn of the century. In 1844, Boole was awarded the first gold medal for mathematics by the Royal Society of London for his paper 'On a general method of analysis', which treated differentiation from the point of view of an operator and exploited its properties. Around this time also he made contributions to the theory of linear transformations.

As a young man George Boole was intensely religious and at one stage even contemplated becoming a clergyman of the Church of England, but difficulties both doctrinal and financial prevented him from following this path. All of his life he viewed the human mind as God's most significant creation, and he set himself the task of understanding how the mind worked and in particular how it processed information. His ultimate ambition was to express the workings of the mind by means of mathematical symbols – this was of course the beginning of a study which led eventually to our present-day world of digital technology, electronics, cybernetics, and high-speed computers.

Classical logic, which in the nineteenth century was not regarded as a branch of mathematics, was the key to Boole's attempt to understand how the human mind processes information. Before Boole's time, algebraic symbols such as x always stood for unknown numbers, but Boole widened this interpretation to allow x to stand for any well-defined class of objects. For example, x could represent the class of all sheep, and y could represent the class of all white objects. Then xy represents the class of all white sheep. In particular, $x^2 = xx$, represents the class of all sheep which are sheep, which is clearly just the class of all sheep! Thus in

George Boole

all cases we get $x^2 = x$, a simple equation which became the cornerstone of Boole's new system, nowadays called Boolean Algebra. He built up the rules to express classes and elementary logical statements in symbolic form, which was a colossal leap forward in both logic and mathematics.

In 1847 Boole published his first book, *The Mathematical Analysis of Logic*, in which he expounded his revolutionary ideas, but unfortunately the book was not widely read. However, as a result of this publication and on the recommendation of many of the leading British mathematicians of the day, Boole was appointed first Professor of Mathematics at the newly founded Queen's College Cork (now University College Cork) in Ireland in 1849. This was a daring move on behalf of the electors considering that he had neither a secondary education nor a university degree, but it turned out very successfully. He filled the chair in Cork with distinction, but not without controversy which included a major conflict over a matter of principle with the then President of Queen's College Cork, Sir Robert Kane, the eminent chemist.

Boole devoted the years 1849 to 1854 busily to his first taste of third-level teaching but also to developing and expanding his work on logic. In his magnum opus *An Investigation of the Laws of Thought*, published in 1854, he made extensive improvements to his earlier work on logic and showed that probability theory is subject to the same laws that govern logic – a most unexpected connection. Boole's book of 1854 has been described by the mathematician–philosopher Bertrand Russell as 'the work in which pure mathematics was discovered', high praise indeed, and the book marked a milestone in the development of logic, probability theory, and mathematics. However, its practical importance and perhaps deeper significance lay untapped until 1938 when the American engineer Claude Shannon at Massachusetts Institute of Technology (MIT) realised that Boole's algebra was precisely what was needed to describe electronic switching circuits and eventually high-speed computers. Thus the modern binary approach to mathematics, logic, electronics and computer science stems almost entirely from Boole's seminal work in the 1850s, as does much of the so-called 'new mathematics' taught to today's schoolchildren.

George Boole made many other contributions to mathematics. He wrote an excellent textbook on differential equations and another on difference equations which was very much ahead of its time in that it foresaw many of the trends towards discrete mathematics which have proved so productive in the twentieth century. Modern legal liability cases, for example, use Boole's method of assigning percentage blame in accident cases. Boole was an excellent and conscientious teacher of mathematics and science at all levels, but he was also a poet and humanitarian, and when in 1857 he received the great honour of being elected a Fellow of the Royal Society, he described his true vocation as that of 'psychologist'. He was actively interested in social causes such as the rehabilitation of 'fallen women', nineteenth-century credit unions, mechanics' institutes, and above all, centres for adult education, which he fostered in both Lincoln and Cork. He was a determined populariser of science and invited many a person into his garden in Cork to view in a spirit of humble reverence the handiwork of God in the heavens through his telescope. Fittingly, in this century one of the craters on the moon has been named the Boole Crater in his honour – he would have been astonished but delighted.

Because of his financial and family circumstances, Boole lived most of his life as a bachelor, but in 1855, at the age of nearly forty, he married a girl just half his age. She was Mary Everest, who came from a distinguished English family. Her uncle, Sir George Everest, was the Surveyor-General of India and the man after whom the world's highest mountain is named. Mary Boole became an educational psychologist, who had many penetrating insights into the teaching of mathematics to children, and her fascinating four volumes of collected works have a surprisingly modern ring to them.

George and Mary Boole appear to have had a blissfully happy marriage and they had five daughters – Mary Ellen (1856), Margaret (1858), Alicia (1860), Lucy (1862), and Ethel (1864). Alicia went on to become an eminent self-taught mathematician; Lucy became the first woman professor of chemistry in England, and Ethel (Voynich) wrote one of the world's bestselling novels, *The Gadfly* (1897). Mary Ellen's son Howard Hinton, FRS, was a famous entomologist, and Margaret's son Sir Geoffrey Taylor, FRS, was a famous applied mathematician. Other descendants of George Boole made important contributions to physics, medicine, sport and art.

Boole's health was never robust and overwork and college controversy weakened him further. He died in 1864 at the tragically early age of 49 as a result of pneumonia caused by walking to a lecture in a December downpour and lecturing all day in wet clothes. He is buried in Blackrock in Cork and is commemorated by the magnificent Boole Library at University College Cork, appropriately the first computerised library in these islands. During his lifetime he received many honorary degrees, such as an LLD from Trinity College Dublin in 1851, and many awards, such as the Keith Prize from the University of Edinburgh in 1857.

George Boole's most enduring contribution to human knowledge was the realisation that mathematics is not confined to the traditional areas of arithmetic, algebra, geometry and calculus, but that mathematics applies to everything – every class of objects, every thought that passes through mind or machine. Everywhere there is order, structure, data or information, there is mathematics. This was a very profound insight, but like all profound insights it was very simple – it could have all been deduced from the trivial observation that a pot of white paint mixed with another pot of white paint gives just a (bigger) pot of white paint. Colour mixing, by the way, such as blue + yellow = green for example gives us another instance of a Boolean Algebra.

Boole's discoveries opened the floodgates and made mathematics central to everything that involves organised thought; but of course Boole did not live to see the fruits of his work. In 1862 he had met with Charles Babbage and inspected his analytical engine, the hardware of which was the forerunner of modern computer hardware. Between them Babbage and Boole had the basis of modern computer technology; if Boole had lived, and he and Babbage had worked together, the digital revolution might have come a long time before it did and history would have been very different.

As it was, Boole's notion that mathematics consists essentially of the manipulation of symbols has had profound effects on the development of mathematics and its applications. Since those symbols do not necessarily have to have a meaning attached to them, they can be processed by minds and machines, which need only to be able to recognise them and process and manipulate them according to specified and prescriptive rules. This is one of the most profound insights ever achieved by a human being and is the essence of the genius of George Boole.

5

George Gabriel Stokes 1819–1903

Alastair Wood
Dublin City University

T HE NAME OF STOKES, a contemporary of Kelvin and Maxwell, has become well known to generations of international scientists, mathematicians and engineers, through its association with various physical laws and mathematical formulae. In standard textbooks of mathematics, physics and engineering we find Stokes Law, Stokes Theorem, Stokes Phenomenon, Stokes conjecture and the Navier-Stokes equations. George Gabriel Stokes has long been associated with the University of Cambridge, where he spent all of his working life, occupying the Lucasian Chair of Mathematics, once held by Isaac Newton, from 1849 until his death in 1903. In this he was like William Thomson, later Lord Kelvin, who is sometimes associated with Glasgow (where he occupied the chair of Natural Philosophy) rather than with Belfast, where he was born. Stokes was born in Skreen, Co. Sligo, where his father was Rector of the Church of Ireland, and received his early education there from the Parish Clerk and later at Dr Wall's School in Dublin. The contribution of Stokes to mathematics and physics was recognised in Ireland with the erection of a memorial at his birthplace in 1995.

The first of the Stokes family to be recorded in history was Gabriel Stokes, born in 1682, a mathematical instrument maker residing in Essex Street, Dublin, who became Deputy Surveyor General of Ireland. Among his concerns was the use of 'hydrostatic balance' to ensure a piped water supply to Dublin. His great grandson, George Gabriel, returned to this problem in one of his earliest papers 'The internal friction of fluids in motion' where he discussed an application to the design of an aqueduct to supply a given quantity of water to a given place. Gabriel's elder son, John, was Regius Professor of Greek and his younger son, another Gabriel, was Professor of Mathematics, both in Dublin University. The descendants of this professor of mathematics became an important medical family in Ireland and internationally. Their name is preserved in medicine through Cheyne–Stokes respiration and the Stokes–Adams syndrome in cardiology. It is interesting to note that George Gabriel, while primarily a mathematical physicist, crossed the boundary between mathematics and medicine by discovering the respiratory function of haemoglobin.

It is from the first Gabriel's elder son, John Stokes, that George Gabriel Stokes is descended. Much less is known about his branch of the family. In 1798, Gabriel Stokes, son of John Stokes and Rector of Skreen, married Elizabeth, the daughter of John Haughton, the Rector of Kilrea. Their first child, Sarah, died in infancy, but they produced seven further children, of whom George Gabriel was the youngest. All of his four brothers became clergymen, the oldest, John Whitley, who was already twenty when George Gabriel was born, becoming Archdeacon of Armagh. In later life Stokes talked fondly of the scenery of his boyhood and his rambles within sound of the Atlantic breakers. Even in his paper 'On the theory of oscillatory waves' he writes, in the midst of mathematical equations, of 'the surf which breaks upon the western coasts as the result of storms out in the Atlantic'. This paper also records a visit to the Giant's Causeway to observe wave phenomena. This very private and reserved Victorian scientist had the occasional habit of breaking into poetical descriptions in the middle of mathematical proofs. In his 1902 paper on asymptotics, he describes what is now known as Stokes's phenomenon as 'the inferior term enters as it were into a mist, is hidden for a little from view, and comes out with its coefficient changed'. Perhaps as a boy he had watched the mists skim the surface of flat-topped Benbulben across the bay, an area which was later to influence the poet W. B. Yeats. There can be no doubt that George Gabriel was greatly inspired by his upbringing in the west of Ireland, and he returned regularly for the summer vacation, a non-trivial exercise in the pre-railway era, while a student in England. Even after the death of his parents he continued to visit his brother John Whitley, then a clergyman in Tyrone, and his sister, Elizabeth Mary, to whom he was greatly attached, in Malahide (where there is a plaque to him in St Andrew's Church) almost annually until his death.

George Gabriel Stokes

Gabriel Stokes died in 1834, and his widow and two daughters had to leave Skreen Rectory, but money was found to send George Gabriel to continue his education at Bristol College in England. His mathematics teacher, Francis Newman, brother of Cardinal Newman, wrote that Stokes 'did many of the propositions of Euclid as problems, without looking at the book'. Stokes appears to have had a great affection for Newman, whom he records as having 'a very pleasing countenance and kindly manners'.

George Gabriel Stokes entered Pembroke College, the third oldest in Cambridge, as an undergraduate in 1837. So effective were his studies that Stokes was Senior Wrangler (that is, placed first in Part II of the Mathematical Tripos) in 1841 and elected to a Fellowship at Pembroke. Almost all of G. G. Stokes's published papers appear in the five-volume *Mathematical and Physical Papers* (Cambridge, 1880–1905). His early research was in the area of hydrodynamics, both experimental and theoretical, during which he put forward the concept of 'internal friction' of an incompressible fluid. This work was independent of the work of Navier, Poisson and Saint-Venant which was appearing in the French literature at the same time, but Stokes's methods could also be applied to other continuous media such as elastic solids. He then turned his attention to oscillatory waves in water, producing the subsequently verified conjecture on the wave of greatest height, which now bears his name.

Such was Stokes's reputation as a promising young man, familiar with the latest Continental literature, that in 1849 he was appointed to the Lucasian Chair of Mathematics. At the same time, to augment his income from this poorly endowed chair, he taught at the School of Mines in London throughout the 1850s. Although appointed to the Lucasian Chair for his outstanding research, Stokes showed a concern in advance of his time for the welfare of his students, stating that he was 'prepared privately to be consulted by and to assist any of the mathematical students of the university'. It is recorded that Charles Babbage, an earlier incumbent, never once addressed classes. Stokes immediately advertised that 'the present professor intends to commence a lecture course in Hydrostatics', which he was still delivering 53 years later, in the last year of his life. Stokes's manuscript notes still exist in the University Library in Cambridge, although his writing was so bad that he eventually became one of the first people in Britain to make regular use of a typewriter.

The mathematical results of Stokes arose mainly from the needs of the physical problems which he and others studied. Besides his links with the School of Mines, he acted, over a period of many years, as consultant to the lensmaker Howard Grubb who ran a successful and internationally known optical works in Rathmines, Dublin. He also acted as adviser on lighthouse illuminants to Trinity House. Stokes's collected works include a paper on a differential equation relating to the breaking of railway bridges and, following the Tay Bridge disaster, he served on a Board of Trade committee to report on wind pressure on railway structures. His paper on periodic series concerned conditions for the expansion of a given function in what we now know as a Fourier series. In the course of this work he made use of what is now called the Riemann–Lebesgue lemma some seven years before Riemann. Stokes is also credited with having had the idea of uniform convergence of a series. His major work on the asymptotic expansion of integrals and solutions of differential equations arose from the optical research of G. B. Airy, where he was the first to recognise what we know today as Stokes's Phenomenon. He employed the saddle point method for integrals in the complex plane a full decade before Riemann, to whom it is usually attributed. The well-known theorem in vector calculus which bears his name is sadly not due to Stokes, but was communicated to him in a letter by Lord Kelvin.

Stokes continued his researches in the principles of geodesy (another link with his surveyor great grandfather) and in the theory of sound, which he treated as a branch of hydrodynamics. But perhaps his major advance was in the wave theory of light, by then well established at Cambridge, examining mathematically the properties of the ether which he treated as a sensibly incompressible elastic medium. This enabled him to obtain major results on the mathematical theory of diffraction, which he confirmed by experiment, and on fluorescence, which led him into the field of spectrum analysis. His last major paper on light was his study of the dynamical theory of double refraction, presented in 1862. After this his time was increasingly taken up with scientific and academic administration.

A major reason for this change was that in 1851 he had been elected a Fellow of the Royal Society and shortly afterwards, in 1854, became Secretary of the Society, where he performed an important role in advising authors of research papers of possible improvements and related work. He acted as a sounding board for many famous scientists, including Lord Kelvin, and was extremely active in the British Association for the Advancement of Science. Many of his colleagues regretted his taking on these administrative duties and P. G. Tait even went so far as to write a letter to *Nature* protesting at 'the spectacle of a genius like that of Stokes' wasted on drudgery [and] exhausting labour'.

In 1859 Stokes vacated his Fellowship at Pembroke, as he was compelled to do by the regulations at that time, on his marriage to Mary Susannah, daughter of Dr Thomas Romney Robinson, FRS, Astronomer at Armagh. Following a change in regulations, he was subsequently able to resume his Fellowship and for the last year of his life served as Master of Pembroke. Shortly after their marriage the couple moved to Lensfield Cottage, a happy and charming home, in which Stokes had a 'simple study' and conducted experiments 'in a narrow passage behind the pantry, with simple and homely apparatus'. Prior to their marriage Stokes, who was a tireless writer of letters, had carried on an extensive (one letter ran to 55 pages) and frank correspondence with his fiancée. In one letter, the theme of which will be familiar to all spouses of research mathematicians, he states that he has been up until 3 a.m. wrestling with a mathematical problem and fears that she will not permit this after their marriage. Based on other remarks in this highly personal correspondence, David Wilson, in his 1987 book on Kelvin and Stokes, suggests that 'Stokes himself may have welcomed what others regretted – his abandonment of the lonely rigours of mathematical physics for domestic life and the collegiality of scientific administration'.

Stokes served as a Member of Parliament for Cambridge University from 1887 to 1892, overlapping with his Presidency of the Royal Society (1885–90). A deeply religious man, Stokes had always been interested in the relationship between science and religion. From 1886 to 1903 he was President of the Victoria Institute, whose aims were 'To examine, from the point of view of science, such questions as may have arisen from an apparent conflict between scientific results and religious truths; to enquire whether the scientific results are or are not well founded'. Many honours were bestowed on him in later life. He was made a baronet (Sir George Gabriel Stokes) by Queen Victoria in 1889, was awarded the Copley Medal of the Royal Society in 1893, and in 1899 given a Professorial Jubilee (50 years as Lucasian Professor) by the University of Cambridge. Stokes died at Lensfield Cottage at 1 a.m. on Sunday, 1 February 1903.

Bibliography

D. B. Wilson (1990) *The Correspondence between Sir George Gabriel Stokes and Sir William Thomson, Baron Kelvin of Largs*, Cambridge: Cambridge University Press.

6

George Salmon 1819–1904

Rod Gow
University College Dublin

G EORGE SALMON ACHIEVED A major European reputation as an original investigator in two disparate fields, mathematics and theology. His mathematical work, which is the main subject of this essay, occupied the first part of his career, and he had essentially ceased to make any significant contributions to mathematics after he had reached his mid-forties. On 22 December 1866, at the age of 47, Salmon was elected Regius Professor of Divinity at Trinity College, Dublin, and he devoted himself to theology for the next 22 years. In 1888, he was appointed Provost of Trinity College, and he served the College with great intellectual authority and wisdom in this office until his death on 22 January 1904. His generosity, which led him to donate several thousand pounds to the College, was marked by the foundation of the Salmon Fund, used to assist poor students at the College. Salmon's time as Provost occurred in a period of great intellectual and social distinction for the College, a period probably never equalled subsequently. The numerous obituaries written about him, in national and local newspapers, as well as scientific proceedings, all testify to his great prestige as administrator, theologian and mathematician. His fame as a mathematician is based on four textbooks that he wrote between 1848 and 1862. These books exerted a great influence on mathematical research and teaching in Europe and America in the second half of the nineteenth century. Each appeared in at least three editions, and his most famous work, *A Treatise on Conic Sections*, has remained in print for over one hundred and fifty years.

George Salmon was born on 25 September 1819. His place of birth has been a matter of some uncertainty, as several articles, some written during Salmon's lifetime, state that he was born in Dublin, whereas other sources claim that he was born in Cork. He was certainly brought up in the city of Cork, where his father, Michael Salmon, was a linen merchant. His mother, *née* Weekes, was the daughter of a clergyman. Through the Weekes family, Salmon was related to Edward Dowden (1843–1913), the critic and Shakespeare scholar, who was Professor of English Literature at Trinity College, Dublin from 1867 until his death. Salmon was educated at the Cork school of Hamblin and Porter, where he received a good foundation in the study of classics.

Salmon matriculated at Trinity College, Dublin, in 1833, and graduated as first Senior Moderator in Mathematics and Physics in 1838, when just nineteen years old. Salmon sat the Fellowship Examination in 1840 and was elected a Fellow of the College in 1841. He was ordained deacon in 1844 and priest in the Church of Ireland in 1845. Salmon married Frances Anne Salvador, the daughter of a Church of England clergyman, in 1844. He lived with his family for forty years in Wellington Road, Dublin. There were six children of the marriage, four boys and two girls, but only two of the children survived Salmon. His wife died in 1878. He is buried with eight family members in a vault in Mount Jerome Cemetery, Dublin, not far from the grave of his famous fellow mathematician William Rowan Hamilton.

On becoming a Fellow, Salmon received a college tutorship, which he retained until 1866. From 1845, he also served as a divinity lecturer. Much of the stimulus for writing his textbooks must have come from the tutor's lectures that he gave during the 1840s and 1850s, as well as the more specialised lectures he gave for candidates for moderatorships in mathematics. Robert S. Ball, former Royal Astronomer of Ireland, described lectures by Salmon that he attended in 1858–59 as follows:

> He was an admirable teacher. I particularly remember the course on conics. It was presumed that we had read or were reading his book, so the lectures often took the line of showing us the improvements or extensions which he was preparing for future editions. He would kindly encourage his pupils to make their comments, and even honour them by asking for their efforts to aid him in questions which were occupying him at the moment.

George Salmon

He used to warn us that the good things were mostly 'threshed out', but still there were some leavings.

In 1862, the Erasmus Smith's Professor of Mathematics at Trinity College, Charles Graves, resigned the professorship. Salmon was the best qualified possible successor to Graves but, as it turned out, he had already decided to concentrate his energies in theology, instead of mathematics, and he never offered himself as a candidate for the vacant mathematical professorship. Instead, a vacancy had occurred in the Archbishop King's Lectureship in Divinity. Salmon had been led to believe that William Lee, who had been appointed Fellow of the College in 1839, would not apply for the Lectureship. This was important, as Lee was certain to be preferred over Salmon, by virtue of his seniority in the Fellowship, if he applied for the position. Lee changed his mind, however, after Michael Roberts had already been appointed Professor of Mathematics, and obtained the lectureship. Four years after this setback, fortune favoured Salmon, for Samuel Butcher, Regius Professor of Divinity, resigned his position to become Bishop of Meath, and, as noted, Salmon was elected his successor, and consequently largely abandoned original work in mathematics.

In the nineteenth century, many mathematicians connected with Trinity College, Dublin, published textbooks or research papers on geometry. Salmon followed in this tradition, and most of his research papers, of which there were about forty, are devoted to geometrical subjects. He was particularly influenced by the book *Traité des propriétés projectives des figures* by Jean-Victor Poncelet, published in 1822. This book laid the foundations of modern projective geometry, a subject first sketched in the seventeenth-century writings of the French mathematicians, Desargues and Pascal. Poncelet's ideas proved to be particularly fertile, especially his use of central projection which showed how the investigations of special configurations of curves could be generalised to much more complicated cases.

What is probably Salmon's most original contribution to mathematical research arose from his correspondence with the English mathematician Arthur Cayley. Cayley had shown in 1849 that a nonsingular cubic surface in the three-dimensional complex projective space contains at most a finite number of lines, and furthermore, that such a surface always contains at least one line. Salmon was able to make Cayley's findings more precise, as he showed that there are exactly 27 lines on a non-singular cubic surface. To this day, the incidence structure known as the 27 lines on a cubic surface, with its associated symmetry group of order 51,840, remains one of the deepest and most intriguing subjects in algebraic geometry. Despite this success, Salmon's enduring reputation as a mathematician does not really rest on his original mathematical papers.

Salmon's real achievement in mathematics lies in the influence exerted by four textbooks he wrote. These were: *A Treatise on Conic Sections* (1848); *A Treatise on the Higher Plane Curves* (1852); *Lessons Introductory to the Modern Higher Algebra* (1859); *A Treatise on the Analytic Geometry of Three Dimensions* (1862). Each of these textbooks was translated into both French and German, and the translations often went through several editions. The German translations, each by the German mathematician Wilhelm Fiedler, were especially highly regarded. The historian of science, J. T. Merz, wrote as follows of these translations and their effect on the teaching of geometry in Germany in the second half of the nineteenth century: 'Germany indeed had not been wanting in original research, but the new ideas of Möbius, Steiner, Staudt, Plücker, and Grassmann in geometry found no adherents till, mainly through the translations of Salmon's text-books by Fiedler, a new spirit came over geometrical teaching'. Later, Merz described Salmon's influence in these words: 'The merit, however, of having brought together the new ideas which emanated from the school of Poncelet and Chasles in France, of Cayley and Sylvester in England, into a connected doctrine, and of having given the impetus to the fundamental remodelling of the text-books and school-books of algebra and geometry in this country [Britain] and in Germany, belongs undeniably to Dr Salmon of Dublin.'

The most famous and enduring textbook, *A Treatise on Conic Sections*, was written for undergraduates at Trinity College, and published in Dublin in an edition of probably 500 copies. From this modest beginning, it passed through five further editions, and became one of the most popular and frequently quoted geometric textbooks of the second half of the nineteenth century. The book contains eight introductory chapters, dealing with the elementary co-ordinate geometry of lines and circles. This part of the book still makes useful reading for beginners in co-ordinate geometry and it is well supplied with examples for study. The next five chapters deal with the three types of conic section, that is, the ellipse, hyperbola, and parabola. The final chapter, on geometric methods, is the most advanced and it is an introduction to the modern geometry developed by Poncelet and Michel Chasles. The mixture of elementary and more sophisticated material seems to have appealed to students, teachers and researchers for several decades.

The third edition of *Conic Sections* was published in London, rather than in Dublin, and this may have ensured that it enjoyed a wider circulation than the first two editions. Its sales may also have been improved by the appearance in December 1855 of a favourable book review in the *Philosophical Magazine*, an important scientific journal. This review was written by Thomas Archer Hirst (1830–92). Hirst was later to become an influential administrator in mathematical and scientific societies, and he was instrumental in securing Salmon's election as a Fellow of the Royal Society of London in 1863. Hirst's review presented various reasons why Salmon's book was so popular. He wrote:

> It is a source of considerable satisfaction to find, amongst the crowd of very imperfect educational books which are daily issued from our press, a treatise so truly valuable as the present; and it is also cheering to learn that the public has so far recognized its merits as to demand a third edition. . . . We venture to assert, that amongst students already acquainted with its merits, this is one of their favourite text-books; for the treatment throughout is admirably clear, strict and elegant, – in fact, such as can be achieved only by one who, besides that perfect mastery of the subject which can only be acquired by original research, possesses also that unacquirable talent of lucid exposition, and is guided by that knowledge of the difficulties usually encountered by students, which experience only can give.

Salmon's second textbook, *Higher Plane Curves*, was published in 1852 in a printing of 750 copies. It was aimed at a more advanced mathematical audience than *Conic Sections*, and was suitable only for senior undergraduates or researchers. It remained the only substantial book in English on its subject for several decades but it seems to have been the least successful in sales terms of his textbooks, since it only ran to three editions, the second not being issued until 21 years after the first. This second edition, published in 1873 after Salmon's withdrawal from active mathematical research, benefited from substantial additions by Arthur Cayley.

Salmon's third textbook, *Modern Higher Algebra*, was published in 1859 in a printing of 500 copies. It deals with the subject of invariant theory, or the algebra of linear transformations, developed initially by Boole, and then more substantially by Cayley and Sylvester in the 1840s and 1850s. A new, much expanded, edition was published in 1866, which was noteworthy for an extensive number of explicit calculations of invariants. There are several vast formulae, each occupying several pages, and one in particular contains 1367 terms and fills thirteen pages. Despite these complexities, the book enjoyed many years of popularity as the best introduction to invariant theory.

Salmon's last textbook, *Geometry of Three Dimensions*, was the longest of his works. It contained, among many other topics, a discussion of his and Cayley's work on the 27 lines on a cubic surface. There was also an appendix on quaternions, applied to geometrical investigations. Hamilton had invented the quaternions in 1843 and it had seemed at one stage in the 1850s that Salmon would become a disciple of quaternionic methods. Salmon's interest proved to be brief, and he never made use of quaternions in his later work.

Salmon continued to write books after becoming Professor of Divinity. These included *Introduction to the New Testament* and *Lectures on the Infallibility of the Church*. Newport White, a former student of Salmon's and later Professor of Divinity, described these books as 'first rank', but opined of Salmon that 'he could not be described as a great theologian. His was not the constructive mind which makes great affirmations on moral or spiritual matters; he was essentially a critic with the instinct for pulling down rather than for building up'.

Salmon's place in the history of mathematics appears to be assured, as his textbooks gained an unusually high degree of recognition for at least 50 years, and in the case of *Conic Sections*, for more than 100 years. His gift was to draw together subjects of current research, display them to the reader, and illustrate the theory by well-chosen examples. Inevitably, a mathematician of a later century who reads Salmon's books will find them lacking in precision and rigour, but his style of exegesis was typical for the time, when the definition, lemma, theorem, proof mode of presentation found in current mathematical textbooks did not exist. Even in his own days, Salmon's textbooks were not free from criticism, for T. A. Hirst wrote in his private journal: 'I had often noticed that his [Salmon's] books, although excellent as a collection of theorems, gave no compact rounded view of the subject, and this defect was at once explained when I learned that he writes his books in a fragmentary manner, beginning to print before he has concluded what shall be the precise nature of the book.' This lack of coherence is least evident in his *Conic Sections*, which is surely the work by which he will be remembered best.

7

John Casey 1820–91

Rod Gow
University College Dublin

ALTHOUGH LARGELY SELF-TAUGHT, John Casey became a major European authority on the modern geometry of the triangle and circle, and he is arguably the most distinguished mathematician who has been associated with the Catholic University of Ireland and its successor institution, University College Dublin. His career as a researching mathematician did not begin until his middle age, and his years working at the Catholic University were fraught with financial insecurity and uncertainty about the future of the university. Despite these difficulties, he brought forth a notable body of research papers and textbooks, at least one of which, *A Sequel to the First Six Books of the Elements of Euclid*, is something of a classic and is still quoted to this day.

Casey's origins seem to have been humble and details of his early life are lacking. There is a short article about him in the *Dictionary of National Biography*, but it contains little that was not already available in obituary notices that appeared in the *Proceedings of the London Mathematical Society* and the *Proceedings of the Royal Society*. While these sources do not agree on the matter, the most likely birthplace for Casey is in the parish of Kilbeheny, near Mitchelstown, which is the town where Casey attended school. His birth date is given, somewhat imprecisely, as May 1820.

Casey became a teacher under the Board of National Education and was eventually appointed headmaster of the Model School, Kilkenny, where he remained until the early 1860s. It is said that he always had an aptitude for mathematics, and this was stimulated into creativity when he was introduced to advanced geometry by a scholar of Trinity College, Dublin, who was dying of consumption in Kilkenny. Casey developed the subject on his own initiative and his proof of a complicated theorem of Poncelet led him into correspondence with two Fellows of Trinity College, George Salmon and Richard Townsend, both of whom were experts on the modern geometry pioneered by Poncelet. These two mathematicians persuaded Casey, at the age of 38, to enter Trinity College to study, free of charge, for a degree, which he obtained in 1862.

While he was a student at Trinity College, Casey became an editor of the first four volumes of the *Oxford, Cambridge and Dublin Messenger of Mathematics*, which were published between 1862 and 1868. Casey contributed several short papers to the *Messenger*, thus embarking on his career as an independent mathematician. His first paper was submitted in October 1861, and it bears the address Model School, Kilkenny. Later papers, written after he graduated, describe him as Science Master at Kingstown (Dun Laoghaire) School. By 1871 he had published thirteen research papers, mainly on curves and surfaces, two of which were substantial contributions of over one hundred pages each. His work at this time was influenced by Arthur Cayley, and also by George Salmon, who mentioned Casey's work several times in later editions of his books.

The year 1873 was to prove crucial for Casey. Presumably on the initiative of Townsend, Casey was offered a professorship in geometry at Trinity College. A little earlier, he had also been offered the position of Professor of Mathematics at the Catholic University. The Catholic University had been founded in 1854 by the Catholic bishops of Ireland, in opposition to the undenominational Queen's Colleges. It had no endowment and its degrees were not recognised by the Government, as it had no charter. By the 1870s it had virtually no students and it was supported largely by collections from Catholic churches. Yet Cardinal Cullen was able to persuade Casey to take the professorship at the Catholic University, to advance the cause of education for Catholics in their own institution. As Trinity College could offer him prestige and financial security, it must have been a difficult choice for Casey to make. A letter from Casey to Townsend, dated 5 November 1873, survives in the archives of Trinity College. In the letter, he thanks Townsend for his support and testifies to the influence of Salmon's textbooks. He does not specifically state why he declined the position at the College, but the final paragraph alludes to the problem of religious difficulties in Ireland. A letter from Townsend to the

Registrar of the College, written the following day, relates that Casey felt bound to decline the position, having already accepted a professorship at the Catholic University.

The subsequent history of the Catholic University is very complicated and cannot be explained briefly. Casey is remembered as one of its few competent teachers, who, in the absence of regular salary, was forced to support himself by grinding students for London University examinations. General dissatisfaction with the state of higher education for Catholics led the Government in 1879 to create the Royal University, an examining body which incorporated the Catholic University and various Queen's Colleges in a loose affiliation. The Catholic University had effectively ceased to exist by 1882, although it still functioned nominally as a grouping of six colleges, and its premises at St Stephen's Green, Dublin, became known as University College. The Royal University provided fellowships worth £400 per annum for a number of teachers in its constituent colleges, and Casey was a recipient of such a fellowship, which must have provided him with some financial security in his last years.

Casey wrote a total of 23 mathematical research papers. One of these, 'On a new form of tangential equation', *Philosophical Transactions*, 167 (1877), pp. 367–440, is unusual among his work, as he made substantial use of calculus, especially the theory of elliptic integrals, in his investigations. The paper attracted the attention of Cayley, who wrote a twenty-page addition to it. Another substantial contribution of 140 pages, *On cubic transformations*, was published by the Royal Irish Academy in 1880 as its first Cunningham Memoir. This work had already earned Casey the Academy's Cunningham Gold Medal in 1878. The title of the paper is slightly misleading, as it really concerns transformations of cubic curves. The influence of both Cayley and Salmon is again evident in the subject matter of this paper. Casey's mathematical researches led to his being elected a member of the Royal Irish Academy in 1866 and a Fellow of the Royal Society in 1875.

By the late 1870s, Casey's interests had shifted from writing research papers on higher geometry to writing textbooks on plane geometry and trigonometry. Showing enormous industry, he published a total of six textbooks between 1881 and 1889, some of which were intended for use as class books in the Royal University, and his reputation as a mathematician rests upon the success and influence of these works. Casey's original textbooks were: *A Sequel to the First Six Books of the Elements of Euclid* (1881); *A Treatise on the Analytical Geometry of the*

Point, Line, Circle and Conic Sections (1885); *A Treatise on Elementary Trigonometry* (1886); *A Treatise on Plane Trigonometry* (1888); *A Treatise on Spherical Trigonometry* (1889). His son-in-law, Patrick Dowling, edited revised versions of some of these books after Casey's death, and they continued to be popular well into the twentieth century. Casey also edited his own version of *The First Six Books of the Elements of Euclid* (1882), which had reached its eleventh edition by 1892. Casey's Euclid is remarkable for its large store of exercises, collected and devised by himself and Richard Townsend, which occasioned the publication of a separate *Key to the Exercises of Casey's Elements of Euclid* (1885). This work was edited by Joseph B. Casey, who was probably a relative of Casey, as the two men shared the same address.

Casey's *Analytical Geometry* was partly an updating of Salmon's *Conic Sections*. The reviewer in the *Freeman's Journal* wrote of it thus:

> Dr Casey's treatise, indeed, may well accomplish for this generation what Dr Salmon's did for their fathers, namely, to introduce the young mathematician to the latest developments in the highest departments of the Science. Scarcely any important step is there in the work which he has not simplified, giving one, sometimes several, original methods.

In the important weekly scientific journal *Nature*, the reviewer observed that:

> Dr Casey, by the publication of this third treatise, has quite fulfilled the expectations we had formed when we stated some months since that he was engaged upon its compilation. He has from the first introduction of certain recent continental discoveries in geometry taken a warm interest in them, and in the purely geometric treatment of them, has himself given several beautiful proofs, and has added discoveries of his own. We may here note that this work has met with a very warm welcome in France and Belgium. The author himself has added so much in years now long past to several branches treated of in the volume now under notice that he is specially fitted, by his intimate acquaintance with it, and by his long tuitional experience, to write a book on analytical geometry.

A copy of Casey's *Analytical Geometry*, annotated in his own hand, is preserved in the Special Collections of the Library of University College Dublin. A considerably augmented second edition of the *Analytical Geometry* was published in 1893, and it is possible to see that several of Casey's pencilled additions and amendments were incorporated into this edition.

John Casey

As was mentioned in the introduction, Casey's *A Sequel to Euclid* is his best monument and it was here that he presented for the first time in a textbook those extensions of the theorems of Euclid that have become known as the modern geometry of the triangle. The modern geometry of the triangle (or more simply triangle geometry) is the study of distinguished points, lines, circles and conics of a triangle. The incentre, circumcentre, orthocentre and centre of gravity are four such well known distinguished points. Subsequently, more than one hundred such distinguished points were enumerated, including the Brocard points, symmedian or Lemoine points and Steiner point. The beginning of modern triangle geometry may be traced to the discovery and study in the early nineteenth century of the nine point circle, a circle with remarkable properties passing through nine distinguished points of a triangle. However, the main impetus for the study of triangle geometry arose in the 1870s from the writings of Emile Lemoine (1840–1912), who introduced the symmedian points. Another important figure in triangle geometry is Henri Brocard (1845–1922), known for the Brocard circle.

Triangle geometry had become very popular as an area of research by the end of the nineteenth century, but it fell rapidly into decline in the twentieth century. Philip J. Davis has described its rise to prominence and given reasons for its eclipse among professional mathematicians in his article 'The rise, fall and possible transformation of triangle geometry: a mini-history', *American Mathematical Monthly*, 102 (1995), pp. 204–14. Triangle geometry remains to this day a fertile source for competition questions among students and for investigations in recreational and non-specialised mathematical journals. Casey's *A Sequel to Euclid* is still a key book for the study of triangle geometry and it is frequently quoted in any literature relating to the subject. The contemporary critical notice in the *Educational Times* was typical of the praise the book received: 'We have certainly seen nowhere so good an introduction to Modern Geometry, or so copious a collection of those elementary propositions not given by Euclid, but which are absolutely indispensable for every student who intends to proceed to the study of Higher Mathematics.' *The Practical Teacher* was equally enthusiastic: 'Professor Casey's aim has been to collect within reasonable compass all those propositions of Modern Geometry to which reference is often made, but which are as yet embodied nowhere. We can unreservedly give the highest praise to the matter of the book. In most cases the proofs are extraordinarily neat.'

Little has been recorded of Casey's life and personality. The few surviving anecdotes suggest that he was a man of simple tastes and pleasures. He was married and had a daughter named Katie, who married Patrick Dowling, a Tutor in Mathematics at University College Dublin and later Registrar of the Royal College of Science in Dublin.

From 1874 or 1875 onwards, Casey lived at 86 Iona Terrace, which is part of the South Circular Road in Dublin and close to Casey's place of work at St Stephen's Green. Casey died of bronchitis on 3 January 1891 and was buried at Glasnevin Cemetery.

8

William Thomson (Lord Kelvin) 1824–1907

Denis Weaire
Trinity College, Dublin

'If one were asked to point out a typical example of the kind of intellect that has changed the face of society so that our whole industrial system has been utterly revolutionised and with it the conditions of life of the majority of civilised nations, the first name that would occur would be that of Lord Kelvin.'

(George Francis Fitzgerald, 1896)

KELVIN WAS A DOMINANT FIGURE in Victorian science. But does he belong in a collection of Irish mathematicians? The world at large regards him as one of the finest flowers of the vigorous tradition of Scottish natural philosophy which for a time outclassed its English counterpart. Indeed he lived most of his life in Glasgow, resisted all temptations to leave it, and took the name of one of its rivers when he was elevated to the peerage. Nevertheless he was born in Belfast and he did not renounce his origins. In a speech in Birmingham in 1883, he spoke 'as an Irishman' in calling for some common sense to be applied to the Irish Question.

Should he be classified as a mathematician? Here again the claim is marginal. Only a fraction of his published output is predominantly mathematical. But the total from which it is taken is so vast (well over 600 papers, many books and over 60 patents) that the mathematical

William Thomson, as a young man *c*. March 1859, reading a letter or letters from Fleming Jenkin about experiments on submarine cables

portion is more than a lifetime's work, by normal standards. He deserves to be called a mathematician, as well as a physicist and even an engineer.

In 1824, when William Thomson was born, his father James was professor of mathematics at the Royal Belfast Academical Institution. This was the forerunner of the excellent secondary school which is universally referred to as 'Inst' in the parlance of Belfast.

James Thomson was of the Scottish Covenanter stock that settled in Northern Ireland in the seventeenth century. His family had a farm in Co. Down until 1847. Talented and industrious, he gained a place in Glasgow University and when later appointed to teach mathematics and geography in Belfast he found time to write textbooks and take responsibility for much of the education of his family. The burden was increased when his wife died, leaving six children. Kelvin, the fourth of them, was six years old. His later expressions of deep gratitude to his devoted father seem well justified.

In 1831, the Thomson family moved to Glasgow, as James had been appointed to the Chair of Mathematics at the University. Remarkably, he allowed William and his brother to attend his lectures. They were not out of their depth. Accordingly they soon became regular students, at the ages of ten and twelve respectively. Both were highly successful, carrying off prizes not just in the mathematical subjects but in the literary ones as well. William soon eclipsed his older brother James, but the latter was no mean intellect, and we should recall his later achievements before he is set aside. He was elected to a Chair of Engineering in 1873.

At the age of sixteen, Kelvin enrolled in Cambridge, at some sacrifice to his father. Why should he do so after so many years of exposure to undergraduate studies? This move should perhaps be considered as analogous to today's postgraduate phase of education, for there was no such thing in 1841, at least in any formal sense. During the previous summer his holiday reading had consisted of Fourier's *Théorie Analytique de la Chaleur* and Laplace's *Mécanique Céleste*. There can have been few Cambridge freshmen that have arrived at their college with such heavyweight intellectual baggage.

Kelvin enjoyed college life, including athletic pursuits. He formed an attachment for Cambridge although he always declined to return permanently, even when offered the Cavendish Chair on three occasions. Foremost among his Cambridge friends was a fellow-Irishman, George Gabriel Stokes.

The statue of William Thomson (Lord Kelvin), which stands in the Botanic Gardens in Belfast.

In 1845 he graduated as Second Wrangler. To have surpassed him in that examination must have been an extraordinary feat: the First Wrangler was Stephen Parkinson, later Tutor of St John's College and author of a treatise on optics. Kelvin did win the first place in the Smith's Prize competition.

Cambridge retained many of its best graduates, as it does today, through the system of College Fellowships, and Kelvin was immediately awarded one by Peterhouse, with £200 per annum.

It had been anticipated by his family that he would succeed William Meikleham, the ailing Professor of Natural Philosophy in Glasgow. Upon his death, Kelvin was indeed appointed and he returned in 1846 to his home and to the position which he was to hold for more than half a century. He was still a young man, but he had already published twenty scientific papers.

He plunged into the demanding business of lecturing to students who enjoyed practical jokes, jibes and other manoeuvres to deflate the professor. In a letter to Stokes he declared one of this first attempts to have been 'rather a failure' because he had read a prepared script too quickly, an experience familiar to most university lecturers. He went on to acquire a reputation as a fine speaker and an inspiring teacher who used practical demonstrations to dramatise his presentations. But there is some evidence that, as with many other intense thinkers, he did not easily find the wavelength of an undergraduate audience. No doubt his mind drifted off into some deep questions in research. A small fragment of one of his lectures survives as a recording.

He had inherited his father's energy and discipline. Combined with his superlative talents, it was enough to conquer the world of science. Eventually his research ranged across all of physics and from the most fundamental to the applied, and its output was spread quite evenly over his long life. He shares with Clausius and Carnot the credit for the Second Law of Thermodynamics, which sets limits on the efficiency of engines. His name is therefore honoured in the modern scientific unit of temperature, the Kelvin, which is closely associated with that law. He also worked in optics, elasticity, electricity and magnetism (under what he called 'the inspiring influence' of Michael Faraday), hydrodynamics, navigation, geophysics, crystallography and the properties of materials.

He discovered with Joule the cooling effect of the expansion of a gas, which was the basis for liquefaction processes. He invented many electrical instruments, and contributed on land and sea to the development of telegraphy, which made him one of the industrial heroes of the age. Faced with all this, let us reduce it to something more manageable by focusing on Kelvin as a mathematician.

The system of competitive cramming for examinations which operated in Cambridge in the time of Kelvin has not entirely disappeared today, being represented by College-organised supervisions. Then, as now, much depended on the quality of this personal direction and assistance. Stokes and Kelvin studied with William Hopkins, the best of the coaches at that time. In addition to the intensive preparation for the contest to come, they were exposed to an atmosphere of advanced research, influenced by both the British and Continental schools. For students of their calibre, lectures were hardly of great relevance.

Within the mathematical tripos there was a wide range of scientific topics, not unlike the list of Kelvin's later achievements, given above. He emerged from this with sharply honed abilities and an appreciation of their possible applications. Thereafter, as Fitzgerald characterised him, he was 'determined at all costs to solve the question', never giving up when confronted by laborious approximations – 'His mathematics is for the sake of the result, and not for the sake of the mathematics'.

The preface to the textbook on physics by Kelvin and P. G. Tait contains a stern warning: 'Nothing can be more fatal than a too confident reliance on mathematical symbols; for the student is only too apt to take the easier course, and consider the *formula* and not the *fact* as the physical reality'.

Even the more abstract notions of theoretical physics had to be given a realistic and concrete form. 'I never satisfy myself until I can make a mechanical model of a thing', said Kelvin. An important example is to be found in the theory of elastic solids. Elegant formal theories had been developed by French mathematicians such as Cauchy. Kelvin's reworking of the whole subject was grounded in the properties of real materials, which led him to reject certain assumptions of the earlier theories and adopt a more empirical approach. With his deep understanding of the mathematical theory of crystallography and his grasp of all the empirical facts about solids, Kelvin could reasonably be called the first solid state theorist.

He also developed new theorems in hydrodynamics, and his interest in the properties of fluids was one of the themes of his lifelong correspondence with George Gabriel Stokes. He became fascinated by vortices and studied them with a view to describing atoms as vortices in the ether. This was an imaginary substance which was supposed to carry light waves as its vibrations. The ether was the source of many mathematical puzzles for him, including a search for an ideal foam structure for it. Mathematically, this was the problem of the division of space into equal volumes with minimal surface area, for which he conjectured the solution.

In one of his letters to Stokes, Kelvin stated what is now known as the Stokes Theorem in vector analysis. It relates an integral over a surface to one around the boundary of that surface. It acquired the name of Stokes when he included it in the Smith's Prize examination four years later, and it became more widely known in that way.

Kelvin also derived much inspiration from the study of his predecessor at Cambridge, George Green. Green had been a miller in Nottingham until he was discovered as a mathematical genius and brought to Cambridge in a famous episode from the history of mathematics. Although elevated to the status of a Cambridge don, Green did not achieve before his death the full recognition he deserved in the wider world. It was Kelvin who drew attention where appropriate to the prior work of Green, when mathematicians began to cover the same ground in later years, particularly in France.

One area in which Kelvin's mathematical talents blended perfectly with his practical bent was in the prediction of tides, for which he invented a calculating machine.

It is probably true that Kelvin got very few calculations wrong, but on some occasions his physical assumptions were inadequate. A famous case was his estimate of the age of the earth, based on its present temperature. Here he understandably failed to include the contribution of the heat of radioactivity.

In addition to his correspondence with Stokes and others, Kelvin recorded his skirmishes with the mathematical problems that he encountered in dozens of notebooks. Scribbled while on visits, travelling in trains, or sitting up in bed in the early morning, they offer a rare insight into the workings of a creative mind. For one thing, they are quite untidy.

Although he eventually became an establishment figure as a trusted adviser of industry and the government, invested with the Order of Merit, Kelvin preferred to stay well away from the 'twin juggernauts' of London and Cambridge. He felt that their many distractions could sap one's energy, which could be better conserved and applied in a place like Glasgow. His record certainly supports the contention, but he failed to persuade his dear friend Stokes that this was the best policy.

He sallied forth regularly to the meetings of the British Association in their heyday, travelling as far as to Montreal to participate in their debates.

On that visit to North America he also delivered his influential 'Baltimore Lectures' at Johns Hopkins University. For many, such pronouncements by Kelvin defined the state of physics in his time.

All of this 'single-minded enthusiasm for truth', as Fitzgerald called it, may convey the impression of a rather dry person. Certainly he was often preoccupied and he had a facility for continuing his rumination in the midst of social distractions, but he had a warm and sympathetic personality, shown in his close family ties and his warm affection for the shy and self-effacing Stokes.

When the Jubilee of his appointment at Glasgow was celebrated in 1896, it was a joyful event. By then he had received innumerable honorary degrees and foreign honours. He had grown rich on the proceeds of his inventions and consultancy and was able to enjoy the pleasures of a large yacht and a splendid mansion by the sea. He had been knighted, then made Baron Kelvin of Largs. In reply to the praises of his many admirers, he characterised his strenuous efforts in the pursuit of science in terms of failure, with a striking humility.

Kelvin lived on to the age of 83, but bad health did not prevent him continuing his work until close to the end, redesigning the marine compass that was one of his favourite inventions. He lost his best friend in science in 1903, and declared that his heart was in the grave with Stokes.

As the last great classical physicist, he had become something of a conservative, reluctant to accept new ideas on radiation or even the possibilities for 'aerial navigation'. But no one doubted the appropriateness of the final ceremony that laid him to rest beside Isaac Newton in Westminster Abbey. As J. J. Thomson said, 'Science never had a more enthusiastic, stimulating or indefatigable leader'.

He left no children, so the indomitable spirit that he inherited from his father was not passed through him to another generation.

Bibliography

A. G. King (1925) *Kelvin the Man*, London: Hodder & Stoughton.

C. Smith and N. I. Norton Wise (1989) *Energy and Empire*, Cambridge: Cambridge University Press.

S. P. Thompson (1910) *The Life of William Thomson*, 2 vols.

D. B. Wilson (1990) *The Correspondence between Sir George Gabriel Stokes and Sir William Thomson, Baron Kelvin of Largs*, Cambridge: Cambridge University Press.

9

Henry John Stephen Smith 1826–83

Rod Gow
University College Dublin

T
HE NAME OF HENRY SMITH is probably now known only to certain mathematical specialists. Even in his own day, the depth and value of Smith's contributions to mathematics were not as widely appreciated as they deserved to be, despite his prominent position in official mathematical and scientific societies and committees. His comparative neglect may be partly explained by his preference for research in advanced subjects, such as number theory, which were little cultivated in British academic circles. He was also notoriously modest, and many of his contemporaries were unaware of his mathematical interests and ability.

Henry Smith was born in Dublin on 2 November 1826. He was the youngest of four children of John Smith (1792–1828), an Irish barrister, and Mary Smith, *née* Murphy, whose family lived near Bantry Bay, Co. Cork. John Smith was a student at Trinity College, Dublin. (A John Smith, born in Limerick, is recorded as matriculating at Trinity College in June, 1810, at the age of sixteen, although this is inconsistent with Henry Smith's father, John, being born in 1792.) After graduating, he was a pupil in London of the lawyer Henry John Stephen, which accounts for his son's three forenames.

On the early death of his father, Henry Smith's mother removed her family to England, eventually settling in the Isle of Wight for much of the 1830s. The Smith family was well connected, as a legacy of £10,000, left

Henry John Stephen Smith

to John Smith by his cousin the Marchioness of Ormonde, was made over to them following litigation, and this money enabled them to live comfortably, both in England and abroad. Henry Smith attended Rugby School for three years, and he won a scholarship to Balliol College, Oxford, in 1844. He gained First Class Honours in both mathematics and classics, and was elected a Fellow of Balliol in 1849. In 1850, he took up a mathematical lectureship at Balliol, and held this position until 1873, when he accepted a fellowship at Corpus Christi College, which relieved him of his lecturing duties.

In 1860, Smith was elected Savilian Professor of Geometry at Oxford University in succession to Baden Powell (father of Robert Baden-Powell, the founder of the Boy Scout movement). Smith's election was noteworthy in that he was preferred over George Boole, then Professor of Mathematics at Queen's College, Cork. Smith was reported to be disturbed at having obtained the position ahead of an older and better established man, but Boole submitted only his name as a candidate, without forwarding the necessary testimonials, and so did not appear to be seriously interested in the Oxford professorship.

Mathematical research, both pure and applied, was popular at Cambridge University and Trinity College, Dublin, during the nineteenth century, but this was not the case at Oxford University. The main subjects cultivated at Oxford in the first half of the nineteenth century were classics and theology, and the greater part of Oxford graduates proceeded into holy orders in the Church of England. Baden Powell (1796–1860) had published elementary treatises on calculus and curves for the use of students at the university, but his main achievements lay in experimental physics, especially optics and radiant heat, rather than in mathematics. There were few distinguished mathematicians working in Oxford during Smith's lifetime and he must have been essentially self-taught as a serious and independent researcher.

Smith's earliest published work was on projective geometry, in the spirit of recent developments in France by Chasles and Poncelet. Smith continued to write on geometry throughout his career and often quoted the books of George Salmon. Later he gave professorial lectures on modern geometry to undergraduates. In 1868, an advertisement appeared for a book to be written by Smith, provisionally entitled *A Course of Lectures on Pure Geometry*, but the proposed book never materialised. This loss was partially rectified in 1893 when J.W. Russell, Smith's pupil and successor as tutor at Balliol, published *An Elementary Treatise on Pure Geometry*.

The reviewer of this work in *Nature*, 1 June 1893, wrote: 'There used to be a rumour abroad that the late Prof. Henry Smith intended to publish his Geometrical Lectures. That hope is now, we presume, frustrated, but as Mr Russell's first lessons in Pure Geometry were learnt from Mr Smith's lectures, and as many of the proofs of the present work are derived from the same source, we must possibly take it as a substitute for the geometrical lectures.' Smith in fact lamented the lack of advanced mathematical textbooks in English and it is a pity that he himself contributed to this lack.

It was, however, in number theory, that Smith made his greatest impression. Modern advanced number theory may be said to date from the appearance of the book *Disquisitiones arithmeticae*, written in Latin by Carl Friedrich Gauss (1777–1855) and published in 1801. In this work, Gauss introduced many of the basic methods of number theory, such as congruence of integers and the use of complex numbers to investigate primes. Smith was greatly influenced by Gauss's work, but he also studied in detail the related work of Dirichlet, Eisenstein, Hermite, Jacobi, Kronecker, Kummer and Legendre, who all worked in France or Germany.

Smith was an active member of the British Association for the Advancement of Science, and frequently contributed to its meetings. He was asked to deliver a report on the current state of number theory to the meeting of the British Association in 1859. The outcome of this request was a series of six reports communicated to the Association between 1859 and 1865 (excluding 1864). Expanded versions of the addresses were published each year in the reports of the meetings of the British Association. These reports were brought together into a single article, entitled *Report on the Theory of Numbers*, occupying 325 pages of the first volume of Smith's collected mathematical papers, which were published in 1894. The entire report summarises and explains much of the work done in number theory to the end of the 1850s. It describes, for example, Kummer's work on ideals, developed to try to prove Fermat's Last Theorem. It also contains original contributions by Smith, and the writing of it stimulated him to publish independent related work elsewhere. To this day, the report makes useful reading for anyone interested both in the historical development of number theory and also in the methods used by the leading researchers.

In 1861, Smith published a paper on the integer-valued solutions to systems of linear equations with integer coefficients. This work was stimulated by his study of number theory. The paper is interesting in that it emphasises matrix methods, such as the formation of the coefficient matrix and the augmented matrix of the system, for solving linear equations, which were quite new at the time. More importantly, the paper is the origin of the *Smith normal form* of an integer matrix, an important concept which has best perpetuated Smith's name in mathematics.

As an indication of Smith's versatility and knowledge of foreign research activity, mention should be made of his paper 'On the integration of discontinuous functions', published in 1875. In this paper, Smith took up the theory of Riemann integration. His main achievement in the paper was to show the existence of a function that is not Riemann integrable and whose set of points of discontinuity is sparse (in the topological sense). In the course of constructing his example, Smith introduced a set of points on the real line which anticipated Georg Cantor's famous ternary set by eight years. Smith's ideas were precursors of the measure-theoretic concepts introduced into integration theory in the early twentieth century. This was Smith's only paper on the subject of integration, and, unfortunately, it was largely ignored until rediscovered later when its true value could be appreciated.

Since the time of Pierre Fermat in the seventeenth century, the question of whether a positive integer is expressible as a sum of squares of integers has stimulated much mathematical activity. The basic result here is due to Lagrange, who proved in 1770 that every positive integer is expressible as the sum of the squares of four integers. Although not every positive integer is the sum of two or three integral squares, Gauss provided necessary and sufficient conditions for a positive integer to be expressible in either form. It follows of course from Lagrange's theorem that every positive integer is also expressible as the sum of five or more integral squares.

Knowing that a given positive integer is expressible as a sum of m integral squares, one may then ask in how many different ways this integer is so expressible. The mathematical convention adopted here is to count the number of *ordered* sets of m integers, the sum of whose squares equals the given integer. The integers used may be positive, negative or zero. A major breakthrough in investigating this question came in 1829, when C. Jacobi published an extensive work on the theory of elliptic functions and theta functions. Using his work on theta function expansions, Jacobi was able to reprove Lagrange's theorem analytically, and, more importantly, he obtained formulae for the number of representations of a positive integer as a sum of four, six, or eight integral squares. Now Gauss had already solved the problem of finding the number of representations of a positive integer as a sum of three integral squares, and Eisenstein had partially solved the equivalent problem for five integral squares in 1847. Smith therefore applied himself to completing Eisenstein's work and solving the problem for seven integral squares. Using intricate algebraic arguments, based on Gauss's earlier techniques, rather than those of Jacobi, Smith succeeded in solving his problems. In his paper 'On the order and genera of quadratic forms containing more than three indeterminates', published in the *Proceedings of the Royal Society* in 1868, Smith outlined his methods, without providing detailed proofs, and gave notice of his intention to furnish full details at a more convenient time. No such details had appeared by 1882, and this proved to be significant during the last year of Smith's life.

In February 1882, Smith read that the subject proposed by the French Academy for the Grand Prix des Sciences Mathématiques was on the number of representations of a positive integer as a sum of five integral squares. As he had already solved this problem, and announced his solution fourteen years earlier, Smith was unsure how to proceed. He was persuaded to submit an entry for the prize, providing complete proofs of his results. Although in bad health, and with little time to meet the deadline for submission, Smith succeeded in presenting his entry, written in French, as stipulated. It is probable that the organising committee for the French Academy expected Smith's to be the sole entry for the competition, so that he could be awarded the prize and his work receive due recognition. This was not to be, for when the results of the competition were announced on 2 April 1883, it was judged that Smith should share the prize with the eighteen-year-old Hermann Minkowski of Königsberg, whose entry had been written in German, contrary to the rules. Furthermore, Smith had already died on 9 February 1883 and so he could not influence events. Something of a scandal briefly followed, when it became known that Smith's priority of discovery was indisputable and an announcement of his methods already in print. Minkowski was even accused of perpetrating a hoax and plagiarising Smith's 1868 paper. After this furore, more measured counsel inclined to the opinion that Minkowski had acted in good faith, and the original outcome of the competition remained unchanged. (Indeed, in the *Dictionary of Scientific Biography*, J. Dieudonné has written: 'Without knowledge of Smith's paper, the eighteen-year-old Minkowski, in a masterful manuscript of 140 pages, reconstructed the entire theory of quadratic forms in n variables with integral coefficients from Eisenstein's sparse indications.

He gave an even better formulation than Smith's because he used a more natural and more general definition of the genus of a form'.) The whole affair of the prize competition and its dual winners reflected badly on the French Academy and did not really give Smith fair credit for his work. Smith's prizewinning submission ('Mémoire sur la représentation des nombres par des sommes de cinq carrés') may be found in the second volume of his collected papers.

Smith was elected a Fellow of the Royal Society in 1861 and served as President of the London Mathematical Society from 1874 to 1876. He was also unsuccessful Liberal candidate for Oxford University in 1878. He was greatly admired by his Oxford contemporaries, who considered him one of the most intellectually distinguished members of the University. He served on various official committees and his opinions were frequently sought for their fairness and good sense. At the time of Smith's death, Mark Pattison, Rector of Lincoln College, Oxford, and an enthusiastic promoter of original research at Oxford University, wrote of Smith as: 'the most accomplished man in the whole university, at once scientific and literary. Twenty MAs – any twenty – might have been taken, without making such a gap in the mind of the place . . . to me it is an irreparable loss'.

It could be argued that Smith achieved less than might have been hoped of him, and a substantial part of his research was never published. This occurred partly because his time was deflected into administrative duties. Unlike many mathematicians working in Britain, Smith kept abreast of work done on the Continent, and he especially admired the profound contributions of the German school of analysis, especially those of Riemann and Weierstrass. Against this he contrasted unfavourably the British mathematical school, with its emphasis on ingenious examination questions, failure to address worthwhile problems, and lack of rigour. For his part, Smith tried to raise British standards nearer to the German level, the only level he considered worthwhile. He was unable to influence the course of mathematical research in Britain, except by his own example, and must be seen as an isolated figure, ahead of his time. He left no school of students pursuing number theory, as might have been the case in Germany, and his only mathematical follower in Britain was James Glaisher, who edited Smith's collected mathematical papers. This work serves as the major source of knowledge on Smith's work and life.

10

Osborne Reynolds 1842–1912

Frank Hodnett
University of Limerick

T HIS SHORT BIOGRAPHY GIVES a flavour of the professional life of the distinguished engineer-scientist Osborne Reynolds. At a very young age he became one of the first professors of engineering in England. As an engineering professor he concerned himself with a wide range of the practical engineering problems of his time. He also sought to understand the basic scientific principles underlying these engineering processes. Through this approach he was able to offer understanding at a fundamental level of many processes in the mechanical sciences. As a result his name is associated with many areas of mechanics, two of which are chosen later to illustrate his influence in their development and understanding. Many others might have been similarly selected. One area highlights his work on understanding turbulence through which the term *Reynolds number* arises. A comprehensive understanding of turbulence, at a fundamental level, continues to this day to be a major active goal of scientific research. The other area highlights his research on understanding thin film lubrication devices in which the Reynolds equation arises. Development of lubrication devices continues vigorously to the present time.

Osborne Reynolds was born in Belfast, on 23 August 1842 and died in Watchet, Somerset, England on 21 February 1912. He came from a clerical family. His father, also Osborne, grandfather and great grandfather were rectors of Debach, Suffolk. His father, the Rev. Osborne Reynolds, was thirteenth Wrangler (ranking in the Mathematical Tripos at Cambridge University) in 1837 and was subsequently Fellow of Queen's College, Cambridge, Principal of Belfast Collegiate School, Headmaster of Dedham Grammar School, Essex, and finally, in his turn, rector of Debach.

Osborne Reynolds, himself, was married twice. First in 1868 to the daughter of Dr Chadwick of Leeds, but unfortunately she died a year later. There was one son from this marriage who died in 1879. His second marriage, in 1881, was to the daughter of the Rev. H. Wilkinson, rector of Otley, Suffolk. There were three sons and a daughter from this marriage. One of the sons graduated in Engineering at Manchester in 1908 and later held the Vulcan and Osborne Reynolds Fellowships. Failing health caused Reynolds to retire in 1905. His retirement years were spent in Watchet, Somerset, where he died at the age of 69.

Reynolds's early education was by his father, first at Dedham and afterwards privately. In 1861, at the age of nineteen, he entered the workshop of Mr Edward Hayes, mechanical engineer, of Stony Stratford, in order, as Mr Hayes expressed it, 'to learn in the shortest time possible how work should be done, and, as far as time would permit, to be made a working mechanic before going to Cambridge to work for Honours'. In October 1863, he was admitted to Queen's College, Cambridge to study for the Mathematical Tripos. The entry requirements included a pass in Greek achieved by Reynolds through 'the obstinate labour of a few weeks' to reach the standard of the 'previous examination'. He graduated in 1867 as seventh Wrangler and was immediately elected to a Fellowship of Queen's College.

Reynold left Cambridge to enter the offices of Lawson and Mansergh, civil engineers in London, but just one year later, in 1868, at the age of 26, he was appointed to the newly established Chair of Engineering at Owens College, which later became the Victoria University of Manchester. He occupied this Chair for thirty-seven years retiring in 1905. This was almost the first chair of engineering in England. That distinction probably lies with King's College, London where William Hosking was appointed in 1840 at the same time as Lewis Gordon was appointed Regius Professor of Civil Engineering and Mechanics at the University of Glasgow. In Ireland the first Chair of Civil Engineering was established at Trinity College, Dublin in 1842 while Chairs of Civil Engineering were established at the Queen's Colleges in Belfast, Cork and Galway in 1849. The selectors for the Owens College chair were highly successful men, distinguished in the practice of business and engineering in the

Manchester area and their selection of such a young and relatively inexperienced engineer seems remarkable. Reynolds's subsequent career proved their choice to be inspired.

Reynolds was of the view that engineering students required a strong scientific training. The course of instruction which he arranged for his students was noteworthy for the thoroughness and completeness of the theoretical groundwork. He was of the opinion that engineering, from the student viewpoint, was a unified whole requiring the same fundamental training irrespective of the nature of the specialisation to come afterwards in practice. He was equally concerned with the practical aspects of engineering and established and developed the famous Whitworth Engineering Laboratories. Several of the more important appliances in these laboratories, such as the triple-expansion engines and the hydraulic brakes, were specially designed by Reynolds for study by students and research, and contained many novel features.

There is testimony that his lectures were not always easy to follow. According to Sir J. J. Thomson, engineering student at Manchester and later Nobel Prizewinner:

> He was one of the most original and independent of men and never did anything or expressed himself like anybody else. The result was that it was very difficult to take notes at his lectures so that we had to trust mainly to Rankine's textbooks [W. J. M. Rankine, Regius Chair of Civil Engineering and Mechanics, University of Glasgow, 1855–72]. Occasionally in the higher classes he would forget all about having to lecture and, after waiting for ten minutes or so, we sent the janitor to tell him we were waiting.
>
> He would come rushing through the door, taking a volume of Rankine from the table, open it apparently at random, see some formula or other and say it was wrong. He then went up to the blackboard to prove this. He wrote on the board with his back to us, talking to himself, and every now and then rubbed it all out and said it was wrong. He would then start afresh on a new line, and so on. Generally, towards the end of the lecture he would finish one which he did not rub out and say that this proved Rankine was right after all.

This lecturing style was redeemed by the personal care and guidance of and friendship offered to his students, which has been generously recorded by many of them. Indeed the illness which compelled his retirement was felt as a grievous personal loss by his students and colleagues.

Osborne Reynolds aged about 24 (*c.* 1866)

There are two aspects to Reynolds's scientific work. As an engineering professor he addressed some major practical engineering issues of his time. These included ship propulsion, pumps, turbines, models of rivers and estuaries, cavitation, condensation of steam, thermodynamics of gas flow, rolling friction and lubrication. But he was also concerned with understanding the fundamental scientific principles underlying engineering processes and hence he developed fundamental theory in a number of areas of the mechanical sciences. Two examples are presented here as illustrations.

Reynolds conducted experiments of fluid flow in long glasses tubes of diameter, d (Figure 1).

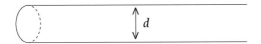

He noted that as the characteristic velocity, U of the fluid is increased (for fixed value of the viscosity, μ, of the fluid) the type of flow changes from laminar (ordered) flow to turbulent (disordered) flow. He was able to demonstrate (in terms of modern notation not used by Reynolds) that the transition to turbulence of flow in a pipe occurs at a critical value of (what is now called) Reynolds number, R_e. The Reynolds number is a dimensionless group given by

$$R_e = \rho d U / \mu \qquad (1)$$

where ρ is the density of the fluid. The critical value of R_e (for transition to turbulence of pipe flow) is approximately 2000.

Turbulence is an extremely important theoretical and technological problem since the presence of turbulence increases resistance to motion; it augments heat transfer rates and general diffusion properties of fluids and gases; it creates noise both directly and through forced vibrations of adjacent structures.

Reynolds gave insight into turbulent behaviour in a simple experimental situation and research on turbulent behaviour continues unabated today since turbulence normally occurs in complicated geometries and in a variety of environments.

From the middle of the nineteenth century industrial advance saw the development and operation of a vast range of machines such as lathes, drills, mechanical harvesters, threshing machines, sewing machines, typewriters, road carriages, railway engines and carriages, which depended for their efficient operation on the lubrication of their moving parts. This technology of lubrication, friction and wear is called tribology. There was concern in industry at the weakness in design of bearings evidenced by failure in operation. This exposed the lack of understanding of the physical basis of effective lubrication. The Institution of Mechanical Engineers were therefore prompted to fund B. Tower to conduct experiments on the operation of journal bearings (i.e. a rotating cylindrical shaft or journal separated from a surrounding cylindrical bearing by a thin film of lubricating oil). Tower reported in 1883 and 1885 (see Dowson, 1987) very considerable pressures, well above the average pressure, in the thin oil film. Reynolds sought to establish a hydrodynamic model for the thin film of lubricant which would yield pressure distributions in agreement with the experiments of Tower. In this he was successful. Reynolds's approach is explained through considering, for simplicity, what is called an aerostatic bearing as shown in Figure 2.

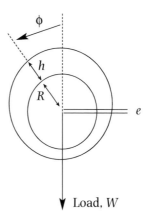

The journal (inner cylinder) carries a load, W so that its centre is displaced eccentrically (from the centre of the surrounding bearing) by the distance, e, called the eccentricity. The radius of the journal is R and h is the clearance between the journal and bearing. In reality (Figure 2 is not drawn to correct scale) h is very small in comparison to R. The circumferential position is given by ϕ with $\phi = 0$ at the top of the journal. If the constant value h_0 represents the unloaded clearance, the eccentricity ratio, ε is defined by $\varepsilon = e/h_0$. Note that ε varies in the range $0 \leq \varepsilon \leq 1$ with $\varepsilon = 0$ representing the unloaded journal and $\varepsilon = 1$ (to be avoided) representing touchdown of the journal on the bearing. The clearance h is given approximately by $h_0(1 + \varepsilon\cos\phi)$. The variation of ε with load, W is what needs to be determined so as to operate at loads giving values of ε away from the touchdown value of $\varepsilon = 1$. Reynolds recognised that in the thin film of lubricant, inertial forces are negligible in comparison to viscous forces and hence derived an equation for the pressure, p, of form

$$\frac{\partial}{\partial x}\left(h^3\frac{\partial p^2}{\partial x}\right) + \frac{\partial}{\partial y}\left(h^3\frac{\partial p^2}{\partial y}\right) = 0 \qquad (2)$$

where x is the distance along the journal (perpendicular to cross section shown in Figure 2) and y is circumferential distance around the journal ($\equiv R\phi$). Note p does not vary across the clearance, h. When the journal rotates, there are extra terms on the right hand side of (2) above. Also (2) is written for the case where the lubricant is a compressible gas. If (as in the Tower experiments) the lubricant is an incompressible fluid then p^2 is replaced by p in (2). Through solving an equation similar to (2), Reynolds was able to reproduce, theoretically, the pressure distribution in the lubricant, found experimentally by Tower. Through equation (2) he offered understanding of the underlying scientific basis for the effective operation of gas and fluid bearings. Equation (2) is called the *Reynolds equation*. Research on and development of thin film lubrication devices continue to be vigorously active to this day.

Acknowledgement

This biography draws heavily on material published in the references given below. The author wishes to thank his colleague Dr E. Gath for help with initial references to Osborne Reynolds and for helpful comments on an initial draft of this manuscript.

Bibliography

D. Dowson (1987) Osborne Reynolds Centenary (1886–1986), *Proceedings of the Institution of Mechanical Engineers*, **201**, C2, pp. 75–96.

D. M. McDowell and J. D. Jackson (eds) (1970) *Osborne Reynolds and Engineering Science Today*, Manchester: Manchester University Press.

Francis Ysidro Edgeworth

11

Francis Ysidro Edgeworth 1845–1926

Anthony F. Desmond
University of Guelph

F RANCIS YSIDRO EDGEWORTH IS mainly remembered today among mathematical statisticians for his development of the so-called Edgeworth series expansion. This topic, rarely encountered at the undergraduate level and not necessarily even at the graduate level, is now experiencing renewed application in the large sample development of recent years. However, recent studies in the history of statistics, especially Stigler (1978, 1986) accord Edgeworth high honours in the late nineteenth and early twentieth-century development of statistics together with Francis Galton and Karl Pearson. Indeed, R. A. Fisher (in his sole reference to Edgeworth in *Statistical Methods and Scientific Inference*) refers to Edgeworth along with Pearson as 'the two leading statisticians in England at the beginning of the twentieth century'. A study of Edgeworth's opus reveals that he made important contributions to the development of significance tests, multivariate normal and correlation theory as well as foreshadowing aspects of maximum likelihood and analysis of variance. Indeed, as pointed out by E. S. Pearson (1967), Edgeworth may have been the first to obtain Student's t-distribution. He derived it, however, via the inverse probability or Bayesian approach as the posterior distribution of the mean of a normal population by a particular choice of prior distribution. He did not attach great importance to it as he realised its sensitivity to the assumed prior in small samples. Pratt (1976) argues convincingly that Edgeworth (1908, 1909) foreshadowed some of R. A. Fisher's fundamental work on maximum likelihood, proving the large sample efficiency, *in frequentist terms*, of the maximum likelihood estimate, although, initially at least, deriving it from an inverse probability premise.

Edgeworth was born on 8 February 1845 at Edgeworthstown, Co. Longford into an illustrious family descended from the Edgewares of Middlesex, who arrived in Ireland in 1585 during the reign of Queen Elizabeth. His aunt was the famous Irish novelist Maria Edgeworth, whose novel *Castle Rackrent* drew on characters from the Edgeworth family. Maria Edgeworth is an important figure in English literature who had important influences on Sir Walter Scott (who was a visitor to Edgeworthstown) and Turgenev, the Russian novelist, whose portrayal of Russian peasant–landlord relations is said to have been influenced by Maria Edgeworth's portrayal of its Irish counterparts. Other visitors to Edgeworthstown included the mathematician Sir William Rowan Hamilton who was a good friend of Francis Ysidro's father. Sir Francis Beaufort (1774–1857), conceiver of the Beaufort Wind Scale and Hydrographer of the Admiralty, was both an uncle and grand-uncle of Francis Ysidro. Another frequent guest at Edgeworthstown was the Rev. Thomas Romney Robinson (1792–1882), mathematical physicist and astronomer in charge of the Armagh observatory. Robinson's second wife was Lucy Jane Edgeworth (1805–97), an aunt of Francis Ysidro. An additional mathematical connection is through Robinson's daughter who married Sir George Gabriel Stokes (1819–1903), Lucasian Professor of Mathematics at Cambridge from 1849. It is possible that Edgeworth's rather late bloom as a mathematical economist and statistician may be due, in part, to these early influences. However, it is known that Edgeworth's father hated mathematics and because of his unwillingness to learn it he did not graduate from Cambridge.

The first members of the Edgeworth family to arrive in Ireland in about 1585 were two brothers, Edward and Francis. Edward was a chaplain who became Bishop of Down and Connor. Francis, whose profession was the law, was granted 600 acres around Mostrim, Co. Longford in 1619, following the policy of James I of awarding Protestants of English descent lands confiscated from Irish Catholics. Later in the seventeenth century Mostrim became known as Edgeworthstown. The early Edgeworths were models for the Rackrents of Maria's famous novel being 'sportsmen, litigants, drunkards, gamblers, duellists and adventurers in marriage' (Butler (1972)). Maria's plot and characterisation for *Castle*

Rackrent were much influenced by her grandfather Richard Edgeworth's *Black Book of Edgeworthstown*, which details the lives and loves of this once very large Anglo-Irish family. Butler and Butler (1927) in a book dedicated to Francis Ysidro give a fascinating account: 'A family saga compounded of debts and prosperous marriages; successive landlords who were selfishly oblivious of their tenants, and yet were strikingly endowed with personal charm, humour and finally pathos.' However, the Edgeworth line from Richard (1717–70) on became prudent, cautious and economical and believed in training future landowners in the law. Francis Ysidro was himself called to the bar in 1877 although he never practised.

The immediate background into which Francis Ysidro was born contained two important influences, the one literary through his Aunt Maria and the other scientific through Maria's father, Richard Lovell Edgeworth (1744–1817). Richard Lovell had many scientific and mechanical interests and was a member of the Lunar Society of Birmingham, whose members included Watt, Wedgewood, Darwin and Galton. Maria's scientific acquaintances also included Davy, Herschel, Babbage, Hooker and Faraday.

Edgeworth's father was Francis Beaufort Edgeworth (1809–46), who was the sixth son and seventeenth surviving child of the last of Richard Lovell's four marriages. Edgeworth's mother was Rosa Florentina Eroles, the daughter of a Spanish refugee from Catalonia. Francis Beaufort met Rosa, en route to Germany to study German philosophy, while visiting the British Museum. Rosa, then aged sixteen, and Francis Beaufort were married within three weeks as a result of this romantic accident. Francis Ysidro was thus of Irish–Spanish–French extraction (the latter through the Beaufort connection). His mixed ancestry and his linguistic abilities in French, German, Spanish and Italian 'contributed to the markedly international sympathies of his mind' (Keynes (1933)).

Edgeworth was educated at Edgeworthstown by tutors until the age of 17, when he went to Trinity College, Dublin, in 1862. Predictably, perhaps, given his literary antecedents, he studied classics, taking first prizes in Greek prose and verse composition. His classical training had a substantial impact on his writing style, so that allusions and quotations from Greek and Latin classics were often sprinkled through his later papers on economics and statistics. His use of analogy and metaphor, a 'charming amalgam of poetry and pedantry, science and art, wit and learning' (Keynes, 1933), makes the title 'the poet of statisticians' remarkably apt.

In 1867, he entered Oxford University, graduating from Balliol with a First Class in Literae Humaniores in 1869. Although a career in classical scholarship might have seemed more probable, he was called to the bar in 1877, perhaps influenced by the tradition of earlier Edgeworths. In 1880 he became a lecturer in logic at King's College, London, a lecturer in political economy in 1888, and finally, Tooke Professor of Political Economy at King's in 1890. In 1891, he became Drummond Professor of Political Economy at Oxford, and was elected a Fellow of All Souls College where he remained until his retirement in 1922. He was a President of the Royal Statistical Society, 1912–14, Vice-President of the Royal Economic Society, and a Fellow of the British Academy. He was the first Editor of the *Economic Journal* and remained an editor from 1891 until his death in 1926. Keynes was a co-editor from 1911 to 1926. According to Keynes, Edgeworth visited Ireland each summer for several weeks staying at the St George Club, Kingstown (now Dun Laoghaire). 'He looked forward to a happy 'old age' in the home of his forefathers'.

Edgeworth was a pioneer in the development of mathematical economics and in the application of probability and statistics to the analysis of social and economic data. His grand objective was to develop the tools originally applied in the previous century by Gauss and Laplace in astronomy and geodesy to the social and economic sphere. With reference to Laplace's *Mécanique Céleste* he writes:

> *Mécanique Sociale* may one day take her place along with *Mécanique Céleste*, throned each upon the double-sided height of one maximum principle, the supreme pinnacle of moral as of physical science. As the movements of each particle, constrained or loose, in a material cosmos are continually subordinated to one maximum sum-total of accumulated energy, so the movements of each soul, whether selfishly isolated or linked sympathetically, may continually be realising the maximum energy of pleasure, the Divine love of the universe.

Edgeworth's first major publication was a monograph entitled *New and Old Methods of Ethics* published in 1877, the same year in which he was called to the bar. This was an attempt to apply mathematical rigour to the subject of ethics by using the calculus of variations to derive conditions of maximum pleasure. This mathematical utilitarianism which he referred to as 'the hedonical calculus' was developed further in a paper with this title in *Mind* (1879, pp. 394–408). Turning from ethics to economics his next major work was the treatise *Mathematical Psychics:*

An Essay on the Application of Mathematics to the Moral Sciences (1881), which attempted to extend the application of the utilitarian calculus to an analysis of economic contract and competition. This book was reviewed somewhat favourably by two of the leading economists of the time, Marshall and Jevons. In particular Marshall wrote that 'this book shows clear signs of genius and is a promise of things to come'. On the other hand, according to Jevons, 'the book is one of the most difficult to read which we ever came across, certainly the most difficult of those purporting to treat of economic science'. Sir Francis Galton, who was a distant cousin of Edgeworth's, disagreed strongly with Jevons's view in a personal letter to Edgeworth, which was highly laudatory. 'It is a grand attempt that you are making and by successive efforts more will assuredly be won.' *Mathematical Psychics* is, to put it mildly, a rather abstract treatise. However, in one of the many appendices entitled 'On the Present Crisis in Ireland', Edgeworth applied his mathematical utilitarianism to the landlord–tenant relationship and defended the landlord interest based on the greater capacity of the upper classes for increments of pleasure. Edgeworth himself had succeeded to the family estate of Edgeworthstown in 1911 after the other heirs had died without leaving male issue. His anti-egalitarian outlook may not appeal to present day Irishmen. According to Keynes (1933), *Mathematical Psychics*, as Edgeworth's first contribution to Economics, contains some of the best work he ever did in this area. It is here that he develops the concepts of the indifference curve and the contract curve.

Following Galton's encouraging letter of 1881, contacts between the two men continued over the years and it is surmised by Stigler (1978) that such contact may have intensified Edgeworth's interest in statistics in the early 1880s. Although *Mathematical Psychics* contains no statistics and only a little probability, in the years 1883 through 1893 Edgeworth's output in statistics and probability was prodigious: almost forty articles and notes, one small book, *Metretike*, and numerous reviews. According to John Venn, in a letter to Francis Galton dated 23 February 1890 (cited in Stigler (1978)), Edgeworth was the leading theoretical statistician at the time. Venn saw the need for a popular treatise on statistics and suggested: 'If it were desirable to go into the mathematical foundation of the various rules, no one would do it better than Edgeworth'. In spite of this, Venn and Edgeworth had fundamental disagreements on the nature of probability. Venn espoused the frequentist theory whereas Edgeworth used inverse probability (i.e. Bayesian methodology) with uniform priors based on the Principle of Insufficient Reason à la Laplace. In 1884, Edgeworth wrote a critical review of the second edition of Venn's *Logic of Chance* entitled 'The Philosophy of Chance' in *Mind*. Edgeworth's views on inverse probability were empirical and pragmatic and were similar to those adopted by Karl Pearson in his *Grammar of Science* (1892). Venn's third edition of the *Logic of Chance* contained substantial revisions, quite probably influenced by Edgeworth, whose help is explicitly acknowledged in the preface.

In the highly productive (from a statistical viewpoint) 1880s, Edgeworth produced important papers on index numbers, significance testing based on assumptions of normality and the use of the 'modulus' ($\sqrt{2}$ times the standard error), goodness of fit, tests for trend in a time series, accommodation of outliers, and arguments favouring the median in estimation of the centre of a distribution. Among the areas of application he treated extensively were psychical research, the mathematical theory of banking, and the reliability of competitive examinations. Other somewhat more exotic applications included attendance at London Clubs, an analysis of frequency of dactyls in Virgilian hexameter and the analysis of traffic rates to and from a wasp's nest at Edgeworthstown at 8 a.m. and 12 noon on 4 September 1886. The data for this latter example, which he collected himself on one of his yearly trips to Ireland, was intended to show by analogy how import/export statistics could be dealt with. He commented:

> If in an insect republic there existed theorizers about trade as well as an industrial class, I could imagine some Protectionist drone expressing his views about 12 o'clock that 4th day of September and pointing triumphantly to the decline in trade of 2½ per cent as indicated by the latest returns. Nor would it have been easy off hand to refute him except by showing that whereas the observed difference between the compared means is only 2, the modulus of comparison is $\sqrt{\dfrac{70}{5} + \dfrac{70}{13}}$ or 4 at least; and that therefore the difference is insignificant.

His work on the statistics of examinations, as described by Stigler (1992), included a discussion of 'how the normal distribution could be used as a scaling device, the virtues of making corrections in the mean for different examiners' propensities, whether or not it was useful to analyse results on a logarithmic scale (or to combine results by a geometric mean), and how to estimate variability (including the introduction of variance components models into this area)'. These ideas were illustrated by empirical data based on his own grading of a set of examinations and also that of teaching assistants. Stigler suggests that Edgeworth, apart from being one of the foremost economic theorists of the time, is also a candidate for the title 'Father of Educational Statistics'.

Edgeworth also foreshadowed Fisher's development of the analysis of variance in a remarkable paper in 1885 'On methods of ascertaining variations in the rate of births, deaths and marriages'. This paper was read at the same meeting of the British Association for the Advancement of Science in which Galton presented his famous paper 'Regression towards mediocrity in heredity stature', in which the term 'regression' is introduced for the first time. Edgeworth presents two applications involving two-way classifications, one to the aforementioned analysis of a passage from Virgil's *Aeneid* and the other to the variation in death rates by year and county. Stigler (1978) gives a detailed numerical commentary and points out that Edgeworth

> presented a method of calculation from which an analysis of variance could today be easily extracted, he gave a way of separately measuring row and column effects that is equivalent to the appropriate F statistics, he considered subtle types of correlation as alternative models to account for large or small values of the F statistics, he gave estimates of error variation based on the error or residual sum of squares and he showed an appreciation of the effect of interaction upon these estimates.

Edgeworth made pioneering contributions to correlation theory and the mathematical development of the multivariate normal distribution in a series of papers in 1892 and 1893. He was the first to derive a formula similar to the modern product-moment estimate of correlation although, as Stigler points out, there was a vagueness about its standardisation; yet Pearson's later treatment in 1896 contained a similar vagueness. Edgeworth wrote to Pearson on 19 June 1896: 'I notice with interest that you obtain my formula for (the most accurate) determination of coefficients of correlation by a different and I think more accurate method than that which I employed.' The modern phrase '*coefficient* of correlation' is due to Edgeworth. In this case as also later in his work on the Edgeworth series, Edgeworth acted as an important stimulus to Pearson, who, unlike Edgeworth, saw the importance of correlation and multiple correlation, particularly in the mathematical study of heredity, and made the most of it.

In his 1892 and 1893 papers Edgeworth also gave the first completely general statement of the multivariate normal distribution, for which he introduced the equivalent of modern notation for the correlation matrix (see Stigler (1986, pp. 322–5)). Pearson gives due credit to Edgeworth in 1895 referring to 'Edgeworth's Theorem'. Later in 1920 Pearson went to considerable lengths to retract his earlier attribution to Edgeworth writing: 'On re-examining his memoir 25 years later I think he harnessed imperfect mathematical analysis to a jolting [*sic*] car and drove it into an Irish bog on his road, and that it was doubtful analysis not errors of printing which led to his obscure conclusions. I was scarcely justified in 1895 in calling the multiple regression result Edgeworth's Theorem.' Stigler (1986) opines that Pearson was unjustified in this matter, pointing out that 'the commentary reflects well neither on Pearson nor upon the general trustworthiness of the later recollections of great scientists'.

Edgeworth and Pearson also disagreed over the analysis of skew (and more generally non-normal) curves and it is clear from their correspondence (see Freeman's discussion of Stigler (1978, p. 319)) that both men were stimulated in a quite competitive sense to do better than one another. Pearson's system won out over the Edgeworth series at the time, although Edgeworth series are now an important tool in modern asymptotic analysis.

Edgeworth's anticipation of aspects of maximum likelihood has already been mentioned but on several public occasions Fisher was reluctant to give Edgeworth much credit. The publication of Fisher's correspondence by Bennett (1990) is of interest in this regard; see especially his replies to Fréchet in 1940 (p. 125) and Gray in 1951 (p. 139), the latter in response to Gray's drawing of Fisher's attention to Neyman's review of Fisher's recently published *Contributions to Mathematical Statistics*. The following quotation from Fisher's letter gives the flavour of Fisher's attitude:

> Edgeworth's paper of 1908 has, of course, been long familiar to me, and to other English statisticians. No one could now read it without realizing that the author was profoundly confused. I should say, for my own part, that he certainly had an inkling of what I later demonstrated. The view, that in any proper sense, he anticipated me is made difficult by a number of verifiable facts.

The modest concession here of 'an inkling', is more generous than Fisher's public utterances. Fisher ends the letter with the following challenge: 'Anyone wishing to ascribe my results to Edgeworth should at least have ascertained that he accepted them, which so far as I know he never did.'

In spite of their disagreements, Karl Pearson and Edgeworth remained on friendly terms, corresponding and exchanging papers until Edgeworth's death in 1926. Pearson gave an affectionate speech at the Galton dinner in February 1926, shortly after Edgeworth's passing. I close with the following brief excerpt which will be of interest to modern statisticians: 'Besides, we owe him something; like a good German he knew that the Greek κ is not a modern *c*, and if any of you wonder where the *k* in *Biometrika* comes from, I will frankly confess that I stole it from Edgeworth. Whenever you see that *k* call to mind dear old Edgeworth.'

Bibliography

J. H. Bennett (ed.) (1990) *Statistical Inference and Analysis: Selected correspondence of R. A. Fisher*, Oxford: Oxford University Press.

J. H. Butler and H.E. Butler (1927) *The Black Book of Edgeworthstown and other Edgeworth Memories 1585–1817*, London: Faber & Gwyer.

M. S. Butler (1972) *Maria Edgeworth: A Literary Biography*, Oxford: Oxford University Press.

J. M. Keynes (1933) F.Y. Edgeworth, in *Essays in Biography*, New York: Harcourt, Brace & Co.

E. S. Pearson (1967) 'Some reflections on continuity in the development of mathematical statistics, 1885–1920', *Biometrika*, **54**, pp. 341–55. Reprinted in E. S. Pearson and M. G. Kendall (eds), *Studies in the History of Statistics and Probability*, London: Charles Griffin, 1970.

J. W. Pratt (1976) 'F.Y. Edgeworth and R.A. Fisher on the efficiency of maximum likelihood estimation', *Annals of Statistics*, **4**, pp. 501–14.

S. M. Stigler (1978) 'Francis Ysidro Edgeworth, Statistician (with discussion)', *Journal of the Royal Statistical Society*, A, **141**, pp. 287–322.

S. M. Stigler (1986) *The History of Statistics: The Measurement of Uncertainty before 1900*, Cambridge, MA.

S. M. Stigler (1992) 'A historical view of statistical concepts in Psychology and educational research', *American Journal of Education*, **101**, pp. 60–70.

12

George Francis Fitzgerald 1851–1901

Denis Weaire
Trinity College, Dublin

W HEN JOHN BELL GAVE a Memorial Lecture on Fitzgerald at Trinity College in 1991, he began by saying that the great man's family circumstances must have been ideal for a career in Trinity College, Dublin. His father had held a Chair there and had gone on to become a leading prelate of the Church of Ireland. His mother was the sister of a distinguished physicist, George Johnstone Stoney. He himself married the daughter of Provost Jellett, who was another scientist.

With all this going for him he could have lapsed into a comfortable academic life, or followed his father into the higher echelons of the church. Instead he devoted himself to a selfless pursuit of the advancement of physics, emerging as the leader of an 'invisible college' of great minds – the Maxwellians. They brought the theories of James Clerk Maxwell to perfection, and applied them to dramatic effect. As historians dig over the ground of late nineteenth-century science, Fitzgerald's reputation continually grows as one of its most inspirational figures.

As in the case of Kelvin, with whom he had much in common (Unionism and a degree of difficulty with undergraduate lectures being two examples), he enjoyed a rather special kind of private education in his youth. He was tutored at home by the sister of George Boole.

Upon his graduation from Trinity College, Dublin in 1871, with the highest place in Mathematics and Experimental Science, he prepared to compete for a Fellowship at Trinity. This required great ability and even greater patience, waiting to fill the shoes of those who departed to vicarages or to the hereafter. In 1877 he succeeded.

He had inherited a marvellous tradition of mathematical physics. One of its strands derived from the work of James MacCullagh, whose attempts to account for the properties of light in terms of the motion of a medium (the ether) were among the most successful in the earlier part of the century. MacCullagh had mysteriously committed suicide, perhaps out of the frustration of being Hamilton's contemporary at Trinity. His work attracted Fitzgerald, and he was given fresh impetus by the advent of Maxwell's electromagnetic theory. This completed the unification of electricity and magnetism, begun by Faraday, by describing them and all their mutual interactions in terms of electric and magnetic fields in space. Fitzgerald consumed the new theory with relish. He saw that it was pregnant with new possibilities and could even free physics from 'the thraldom of a material ether', although he continued to use the word ether, rather than the modern terminology of the electromagnetic field. He was to devote the rest of his life to this new kind of ether and its interaction with matter.

In 1881 he was appointed as Erasmus Smith Professor of Natural and Experimental Philosophy, and this was quickly followed by election to the Royal Society. Larmor later recalled that he was 'the idol of the undergraduates and the hope of the older men' at that time.

Determined to introduce the teaching of practical physics, he took possession of an old chemical laboratory. This was the beginning of a long campaign for proper experimental facilities, not just for himself but for applied science throughout Ireland. He was outraged when the government equipped the new Royal University (set up to provide degree examinations for small, mostly Catholic, institutions) with the very latest spectroscopic facilities. He eventually succeeded in getting his college to provide decent accommodation for physics, but the Physical Laboratory was not built until after his death. In justice, it should be called the Fitzgerald Building.*

In his concern for practical applications he again mirrors the career of Kelvin, but to less effect. He had the same realistic approach, demanding mechanical models to demonstrate the validity of theories. He made one to represent the Maxwell theory – it has unfortunately been lost in recent times.

* Between the writing of this chapter and its publication, Trinity College has approved and implemented the renaming of the building.

George Francis Fitzgerald

One of the important implications that he saw in Maxwell's theory was the generation of electromagnetic waves by an oscillating electrical circuit. Could this be accomplished in practice? He was somewhat unsure about this, changing the title of one paper from 'Impossibility . . .' to 'Possibility . . .' at a late stage. His line of thought was triumphantly vindicated by the 1887 experiment of Hertz, which generated the radio waves that he had anticipated. No wonder that Fitzgerald waxed lyrical, in the climax to his interpretation of this breakthrough before the British Association in 1888: 'it is only within the last few years that man has won the battle lost by the giants of old, has snatched the thunderbolt from Jove himself and enslaved the all-pervading ether'.

During this period there was a rich ferment of new ideas, shared and debated by the Maxwellians. They included Hertz, Larmor, Heaviside, Lodge and others. Fitzgerald was their acknowledged leader and the source of many of their ideas, but he made few claims and wrote comparatively little. In part this was because he was increasingly preoccupied with such matters as public policy in technical education.

In early 1889 he was visiting his good friend and fellow Maxwellian, Oliver Lodge, in Liverpool. They discussed the Michelson–Morley experiment, which had failed to find any effect of the motion of the earth through the ether, when the speed of light was measured in different directions. Suddenly he had an idea, that the dimension of a moving body could be altered by its motion – this could account for the experiment. He sent a short paper to an obscure American journal (*Science*) and proceeded to forget about it. Only when Lorentz published the same hypothesis did Fitzgerald recall that paper; he had never seen it in print.

Today the effect is called after both men, and is a standard feature of the theory of special relativity. As John Bell has explained, it is wrong to consider this just a wild guess, a shot in the dark. The mathematical formulae for the electromagnetic field that Fitzgerald had been scrutinising with the Maxwellians contained the clues to length contraction.

Not only did Fitzgerald presage this aspect of relativity theory, but he also remarked that it might well be that no body could exceed the speed of light, since this had unpleasant consequences for electromagnetic theory. He appears to have been the first to recognise this limitation, which again has its place in the theory of relativity.

In a letter to Oliver Heaviside, Fitzgerald apologised for this tendency to throw out fragmentary thoughts (though Heaviside was a far greater eccentric than he): 'I admire from a distance those who contain themselves till they worked to the bottom of their results but as I am not in the very least sensitive to having made mistakes I rush out with all sorts of crude notions in hope that they may set others thinking and lead to some advance.'

In the 1890s the Erasmus Smith Professor enjoyed rather more support, in the form of an Assistant and others who became associated with the Department, perhaps attracted by the Experimental Science Association, in which he played a leading role. Practical devices, such as a Gramme dynamo were exhibited and operated at these meetings, together with accounts of the latest discoveries.

One of his demonstrations required special facilities in College Park, when he attempted to fly the Lilienthal glider. He was the first to do so in the British Isles. There is no evidence of his having gained any great height. This may have been owing to a physicist's intuition of the problems of stability. Others, including Otto Lilienthal, were to give their lives in trying the glider. Because of his caution, he had to bear the title Flightless Fitzgerald in the College thereafter.

Among those inspired by his leadership at that time were:

- E. E. Fournier D'Albe, who wrote the first popular book on the electron, and was a pioneer inventor in the advent of television;

- John Joly, the leader in the study of radioactivity in geology, who made an astonishing number of inventions during the period in which he was associated with Fitzgerald;

- Thomas Preston, discoverer of the Anomalous Zeeman Effect in experiments conducted at the Royal University of Ireland, and author of excellent textbooks on Light and Heat;

- Frederick Trouton, who formulated Trouton's Rule in physical chemistry;

- Thomas Ranken Lyle, father figure of physics in Australia.

In addition, the Maxwellians had expanded into an even wider circle of correspondents, who wrote to Fitzgerald in the sure expectation of a generous and authoritative (if not always correct) response, and offer of assistance. He helped W. H. S. Monck make the first photoelectric measurements of starlight in 1892.

One regular correspondent was his uncle, George Johnstone Stoney, now remembered for having given the electron its name. This grand old

Fitzgerald attempting to fly the Lilienthal glider in College Park of Trinity College, Dublin, in the 1890s.

man of science once complained to Fitzgerald about the impertinence of young Thomas Preston:

> Another feature which then distinguished the teaching of the University of Dublin in Mathematical Physics was the almost exclusive study of great writers – Newton, Lagrange, Laplace, Poisson, Gauss, MacCullagh, Ampere etc – instead of re-castings of their work by compilers of textbooks; and all were illuminated by incorporating into them the geometrical methods peculiar to the University, wherever this was practical. The great achievements of the fifty years that have elapsed – Thermodynamics: the Kinetic Theory of gas; Spectroscopy; the Electricity of Faraday, and Lord Kelvin; the Electromagnetic theory of light – were then unknown; but while the teaching of the University has since gained so immensely, something has been lost, and especially in regard to the methods which were distinctive of a Dublin training and which in a marked degree tended to produce original thinkers.

It was said that, in the end, all this led to overwork. He died in 1901; the diagnosis was a stomach ulcer. Joseph Larmor collected his publications (but not all – at least thirty are missing from the published *Scientific Writings*), together with anguished tributes from those who had benefited so much from Fitzgerald's influence.

The eulogy by Lodge is the most revealing in regard to the great man's temperament, saying that he was 'impulsive, hot-tempered and totally unselfconscious; he alternated between abstract meditation, highly individual experimentation and passionate advocacy of his favorite causes'. Valentine Ball summed this up as his 'perfervid genius'. The folk tales of Trinity include one in which Fitzgerald pulled a knife on another Fellow whose inanities he could no longer stand. But at heart he was full of generosity: it was he who instigated and led the successful campaign to persuade the government to grant Oliver Heaviside a small pension, to save that wayward genius from ending his days in obscure poverty.

As for the mark that he had left on science, it was registered by the distinction of an extended obituary in the American journal *Physical Review*. Sadly, the previous entry had been that of his star pupil, Thomas Preston, whose last letter to Fitzgerald called him his 'mentor and constant friend'. The two men died after similar illnesses and one is bound to wonder whether they were martyrs to the reckless use of x-ray sources which was common at that time.

A mass of correspondence survived and is currently being edited, together with a number of his personal notebooks and an unfinished textbook manuscript. His glider also survived on display in Trinity, until an engineering student applied a match to a cord which dangled from it . . . .

Perhaps, in the end, Fitzgerald could be considered as a Kelvin *manqué*. No knighthood came his way, and he felt neglected by the government. But he did surpass his Glasgow counterpart in one respect, leaving five daughters and three sons.

Bibliography

B. Hunt (1991) *The Maxwellians*, Ithaca NY: Cornell University Press.
J. Larmor (ed.) (1902) *The Scientific Writings of George Francis Fitzgerald*, Dublin: Hodges Figgis.

13

Edmund Taylor Whittaker
1873–1956

David H. Armitage
The Queen's University of Belfast

T HROUGHOUT THE FIRST HALF of the twentieth century E. T. Whittaker made important original contributions to several branches of mathematics and mathematical physics. He also wrote extensively and authoritatively on the history of science and the impact of science on philosophy and theology. He lived only six years in Ireland, quite early in his long career, but he maintained links with the country throughout his life and profoundly influenced the development of science in Ireland.

His Whittaker forebears came from the Ribble Valley in north-west England. Several members of the family attained positions of rank and influence in Victorian times, notably Sir Thomas Palmer Whittaker (1850–1919), for many years MP for Spen Valley, Yorkshire, and Sir Meredith T. Whittaker (1841–1931) of Scarborough. Edmund Taylor Whittaker was born on 24 October 1873, the eldest child of John Whittaker, railway engineer and contractor, and his wife Selina, daughter of Edmund Taylor, a physician practising in Middleton near Manchester. On their marriage, John and Selina settled in Birkdale near Southport on the Lancashire coast, where Edmund was born and brought up. In his early years his health was delicate and he was educated at home by his devoted mother.

The boy's health improved, and at the age of eleven he was sent away to Manchester Grammar School, where he started as a classical specialist, spending 60 per cent of his time on Latin and Greek. At first the work was purely linguistic and he did well, but poetry and drama were not to his taste, and on promotion to the upper school he changed his specialisation to mathematics.

In 1891 Whittaker was awarded an entrance scholarship to Trinity College, Cambridge. The following year he entered the University, where he was a pupil of G. H. Darwin and A. R. Forsyth. As an undergraduate, Whittaker was mainly interested in applied mathematics, and he won the Sheepshanks Exhibition in astronomy in 1894. In the tripos of 1895, he was joint Second Wrangler with J. H. Grace; the Senior Wrangler was T. J. l'A. Bromwich.

Whittaker was elected a Fellow of Trinity College in 1896 and immediately began giving lectures. Among his courses was one on analysis. At that time the great advances in analysis made by continental mathematicians were only slowly gaining recognition in Cambridge, the centre of the British mathematical world. But change was under way: Forsyth's *Theory of Functions of a Complex Variable* (1893) had, according to Whittaker, 'perhaps a greater influence on English mathematics than any work since Newton's *Principia*'. J. E. Littlewood disagreed: 'this is the sort of thing my generation had to go through', he later wrote of Forsyth's two-page attempt to define a regular function. However, there is no doubt about the lasting value of Whittaker's own work, *A course of modern analysis: an introduction to the general theory of infinite series and analytic functions; with an account of the principal transcendental functions.* First published in 1902, it was based on his lectures and is now known simply as 'Whittaker and Watson'. G. N. Watson, who studied under Whittaker, shared the preparation of the second edition (1915) which made good some inadequacies in the original text and added about 200 pages in new chapters. Further editions came out in 1920 and 1927, and the book has been regularly reprinted throughout the century. It continues to be used as a reference work on the higher transcendental functions.

As well as lecturing on analysis, Whittaker taught a range of courses in 'natural philosophy': for instance Astronomy, Geometrical Optics, and Electricity and Magnetism. His students included men who were to attain greatness, notably the mathematicians G. H. Hardy and J. E. Littlewood, and the cosmologists A. S. Eddington and J. H. Jeans. One of his students, H. W. Turnbull, gives us a picture of Whittaker as a young man – 'He saw in this learned man a slight figure, with a moustache, bespectacled, and an easy manner of speaking, a curious mixture of precision and grace,

Edmund Taylor Whittaker

never at a loss, always moving with deceptive ease through his subject, making it at once a logical structure and work of art.'

Much of Whittaker's early published work was concerned with dynamics. As early as 1898 the Council of the British Association resolved that he 'be requested to draw up a report on the planetary theory'. His *Report on the progress of the solution of the problem of three bodies* duly appeared the following year, and the famous three-body problem was a major theme in his large-scale treatise on analytical dynamics of 1904. In those years it was not uncommon for mathematicians to take a serious interest in astronomy, and many were members of the Royal Astronomical Society. Whittaker was the Society's secretary from 1901 to 1906.

C. J. Joly, Royal Astronomer of Ireland and Andrews' Professor of Astronomy in the University of Dublin (Trinity College), died at the age of 41 early in 1906. Within two months Whittaker had been nominated as Joly's successor, and he took up his duties on 21 June. He had married Mary Boyd, daughter of the Rev. Thomas Boyd of Edinburgh, on 7 August 1901, and by the time of his appointment they had two children. Two more were born while they were at Dublin, and a fifth subsequently. The family was provided with a pleasant house with a large garden, near Dunsink Observatory, about seven miles from Dublin. This was ideal for the young family and for Whittaker himself, as gardening was his main hobby apart from his intellectual interests.

Whittaker's teaching duties were light, at least by comparison with those of his Cambridge years; each year he gave one or two postgraduate courses on astronomical topics. J. J. Dowling (later a professor at University College Dublin) attended Whittaker's lectures in 1907–8 and recalled that they 'were given on winter evenings in a room in Trinity College that had a narrow wall-blackboard about twenty feet long. Whittaker, with only a few formulae on a postcard by way of notes, wrote every word of his lecture on the board, running back to the other end of the board after finishing each line. The performance, which always ended on time, left Whittaker perspiring and his audience dazed but evidently still enthusiastic'. Much later accounts of Whittaker's lecturing style confirm that everything was written on the board but he referred to complete sets of notes. One of his courses formed the basis of his Cambridge Tract, *The theory of optical instruments*. Other courses contributed to his classical *History of the theories of aether and electricity from the age of Descartes to the close of the nineteenth century*, published in 1910.

Dunsink Observatory's brief annual report for 1911 records that the staff consisted of Whittaker (Director) and a single Assistant, Mr C. Martin, and states that 398 plates were taken in connection with the observing list of variable stars. Only two of Whittaker's research papers deal with actual astronomical observations; other papers from his time in Dublin are on topics in theoretical astronomy.

Open nights were held at the Observatory on the first Saturday of each month. A *Visitors' Book* running from 17 July 1906 to 20 April 1912 (roughly Whittaker's period in office) includes the name of Eamon de Valera of 'University College, Blackrock' on 5 June 1909. De Valera had been a student of Whittaker's, and through their friendship Whittaker made an enduring contribution to science in Ireland. Many years after their first acquaintance, during the Second World War, de Valera consulted Whittaker about his plans for the School of Theoretical Physics in the Dublin Institute for Advanced Studies, and Whittaker became one of its first Board Members, although the war prevented him from travelling to Dublin for meetings. The sort of advice that Whittaker gave may be gleaned from a draft letter of his, dated 5 December 1942, beginning 'Dear Taoiseach'. The draft sets out several carefully reasoned suggestions and ends ambitiously and optimistically:

> I ought perhaps to express my opinion that at present and in the imme-diate future the institution which will – to put it crudely – give the Irish Government the best return for modest expenditure is the Institute for Theoretical Physics. This is an illustration of the principle I mentioned above, that the Institute should be created for the man; for it is the fortunate circumstance that Schrödinger and Heitler were available that accounts for the wonderful success of the Institute. When the war ends, it would be possible to attract to Dublin every brilliant young theoretical physicist from an impoverished and starving Europe, if the Irish Government were willing to allocate a sum for research studentships for them. The very best of them could be kept and so the life of the Institute could be maintained at the highest level, as perhaps the chief centre for this important subject in the world.

In 1912 Whittaker succeeded George Chrystal as Professor of Mathematics in the University of Edinburgh, where he soon began to take radical initiatives. A mathematical laboratory, the first of its kind in Britain, was opened in October 1913 for teaching and research in various branches of computational mathematics. Another innovation of his was the series of research lectures which he gave twice weekly, with the purpose of drawing attention to questions ripe for investigation and thus fostering research within the department. Whittaker took a special interest in the teaching of actuarial mathematics; in this he was continuing work begun by Colin Maclaurin who had occupied the same Chair (1725–46) in a city with a long history as a centre for life assurance. Many excellent staff appointments were made. Typically a young mathematician would be brought in from another university, spend a few productive years in Edinburgh, and then move to a senior post elsewhere. Among staff who obtained chairs were A. C. Aitken (E. T. W.'s successor at Edinburgh), B. Baker, E. T. Copson (a son-in-law of E. T. W.), L. R. Ford, W. H. McCrea, H. S. Ruse and J. M. Whittaker (second son of E. T. W.).

Whittaker had no special taste for administrative work but he conceived it as part of his duty to see that his department's interests were properly represented, and he played a prominent role in the councils of the University, eventually serving for a period as its Acting Principal.

During the years around the First World War, Whittaker published widely in pure mathematics. Recurring themes are differential and integral equations and special functions, and there are also papers on determinants and continued fractions. Much of his work in the 1920s is concerned with mathematical physics, especially electromagnetism in the context of relativity, and has a geometrical cast. From about 1930 his purely scientific output started to wane, but he wrote extensively about the history of science and on philosophical and theological questions.

The Second World War altered the course of Whittaker's life. He had intended to spend his retirement in Dublin, but having attained the statutory age of 70 in 1943, he volunteered to stay on until he could hand over to his successor in peacetime. He eventually retired in 1946, by which time he felt it was too late to make a new home. In retirement he continued to pursue his intellectual interests. His *History of the Theories of Aether and Electricity* (1910), which covered the years up to 1900, was revised and published in 1951, intended as the first volume of a trilogy. The second volume, dealing with the crucial period 1900–26, appeared in 1953, and the third volume, 1926–50, was in preparation at the time of his death. Whittaker was uniquely qualified for this huge undertaking: educated near the end of the classical period, he had lived through and contributed to the revolution in physics; he had personally known leading physicists from Kelvin, Fitzgerald, Larmor, Lorentz and J. J. Thomson onwards. Throughout his life, Whittaker was deeply religious and read widely in Christian theology. Having belonged at different times to a number of Protestant denominations, he was received into the Catholic Church in 1930. Much of his later writing was at the interface of cosmology and theology. His Donnellan Lectures, given in Dublin in 1946, for instance, examine the possible repercussions of modern science on traditional arguments from reason for the existence of God; the lectures were published the following year under the title *Space and Spirit*. Public lectures at Durham, Oxford and Cambridge around the same period were also about historical, philosophical and theological issues. In his last years, he gave some semi-popular radio talks and was, we are told, a first-class speaker.

Whittaker received numerous honours from learned societies, universities, Church, and State. He was elected FRS in 1905 and was awarded the Sylvester Medal (1931), the de Morgan Medal (1935), and the Copley Medal (1954). He received a knighthood in 1945. At various times he was President of the London Mathematical Society, the Royal Society of Edinburgh, the Mathematical Association, and Section A of the British Association. He held honorary degrees of seven universities and was an honorary member of several foreign academies. His final honour was his election as corresponding member of the Académie des Sciences (Section de Géométrie) on 12 March 1956. He died in Edinburgh twelve days later, survived by Lady Whittaker, his wife for fifty-four and a half years, and their three sons and two daughters.

14

William Sealy Gosset – alias 'Student' 1876–1937

Philip J. Boland
University College Dublin

WILLIAM SEALY GOSSET ESTABLISHED his place in the history of scientific method through the development of *Student's t-test*, a statistical test of significance developed for work in Guinness Breweries, but which is now commonly used daily in almost all areas of scientific research. Gosset was born in Canterbury on 13 June 1876, the first of five children of Colonel Frederic Gosset and Agnes Sealy Vidal. Although he was not able to follow his father in the Royal Engineers because of poor eyesight, he was a good student and won various scholarships. He was a scholar at New College, Oxford where he obtained a first in Mathematical Moderations in 1897, and he left Oxford with a First Class degree in Chemistry in 1899. At about this time Arthur Guinness, Son & Co. in Dublin decided to try to incorporate new scientific methods into its brewing process, and as a result was in the market to hire bright young science graduates to help in this direction. Gosset was one of the first such scientists, and in 1899 he moved to Dublin to take up a job as a brewer at St James's Gate. In 1906 he married Marjory Surtees Phillpotts, the sister of his friend and fellow Guinness 'brewer' Geoffrey Phillpotts, with whom he had three children and lived in Blackrock, Co. Dublin. He left Dublin in 1935 to become head brewer at the new Park Royal Brewery of Guinness in London, but died shortly thereafter in 1937. The great statistician and mathematician R. A. Fisher, in his tribute to 'Student' in 1939, wrote, 'The untimely death of W. S. Gosset, at the age of 61, in October 1937, has taken one of the most original minds in contemporary science'.

In his initial years at St James's Gate, Gosset familiarised himself with various aspects of the brewing process and in 1904 he wrote a report for Guinness on 'The Application of the Law of Error to Work of the Brewery'. In the report Gosset emphasised the importance of probability in the setting of exact values for the results of experiments in the brewery. Although much of the report was an application of the classical theory of errors to work being carried out at St James's Gate, it also demonstrated a curious mind at work delving into new horizons. One recommendation in the report was that a mathematician should be consulted with respect to special problems in analysing 'small' samples that resulted from experiments in the brewery. As a result, Gosset came in contact with Karl Pearson (1857–1936), an industrious and brilliant man of many talents who at the time headed the biometric laboratory at University College London. In 1906 he obtained a year's leave of absence to spend at Pearson's laboratory in London, and here he obtained the statistical foundations necessary for much of his future work at Guinness. In particular he was introduced to correlation coefficients and the large sample theory which was extensively used by biometers at the time. He was aware, however, that modifications of Pearson's methods which were based on large samples of data would be necessary in order to deal with the special small sample problems that arose in the brewery. Gosset was a very practical man, and most of the statistical methods that he developed were in response to problems in the brewery dealing with the production of stout and arising from variations in barley, hops, malt and other experimental conditions.

William Sealy Gosset published 22 scientific papers, all written under the modest pseudonym of 'Student'. Arthur Guinness, Son & Co., which during Gosset's time was well ahead of the field in applications of scientific methods to brewing, placed considerable emphasis on secrecy in order that no important information was given to its competitors. The company was therefore not keen on its employees publishing scientific discoveries, and, when necessary, pseudonyms were to be used. Another consequence of this was that prior to the Second World War, Guinness took little part in any of the Brewing/Scientific societies (Smith, 1987).

Gosset's first publication was 'On the Error of Counting with a Haemacytometer', which appeared in Karl Pearson's journal *Biometrika* in 1906. In this paper he addressed the problem of the distribution of

William Sealy Gosset

particles throughout a liquid, with particular reference to the counting of yeast cells or blood corpuscles in a liquid spread thinly over a grid. He developed an 'exponential series' as a limit to the binomial distribution and showed that this series modelled well the distribution of small particles in a liquid. Gosset was in fact unaware that he had 'rediscovered' the Poisson distribution, but he made a valuable contribution in giving new practical applications for this probability distribution.

Gosset's greatest contribution to statistics arose from his second publication entitled 'On the Probable Error of a Mean', which appeared in *Biometrika* in 1908. Like many other scientists at the time, Gosset was interested in how the mean of a sample might vary about the mean of a given population in an experiment. It was well known that the normal distribution (normal tables) was able to give trustworthy answers when the samples were large, but Gosset was primarily concerned with small samples arising from work in the brewery. This led Gosset to furnish alternative tables for use when the sample size was small. This was truly a landmark paper in the history of statistics. It was well written and motivated, and was one of the first papers to make a clear distinction between population parameters (like the mean μ and standard deviation σ) and sample estimates of them (respectively $\bar{x}$ and s). Gosset derived (although his insight was uncanny, his proof was slightly lacking in mathematical rigour) the probability distribution of the standardised version of the sample mean given by $z = (x - \mu)/s$, and gave tables for his z distribution. He empirically checked the adequacy of his distribution on a data set consisting of the height and left middle finger length of 3000 criminals. In the process of doing so (where he took small samples of size 4) he was one of the first researchers to use simulation in statistical research. Furthermore, he gave four practical examples of his method (from agriculture and pharmacology, but not from work in the brewery as this was not permitted by Guinness).

As there was little interest in 'small sample' statistics at the time, Gosset's work on the z distribution had little impact outside the brewery for many years. Eventually of course it became (in modified form) extensively used, mainly through the promotional efforts of R. A. Fisher who is generally regarded as having made the greatest contributions to the development of modern statistics. R. A. Fisher (see Conniffe (1990/1991) for an interesting commemoration to Fisher in his Centenary year) was a student at Cambridge in 1912 when he wrote to Gosset with a rigorous mathematical treatment of the z distribution in terms of transformations in *n*-dimensional Euclidean space. Although Gosset's classic 1908 paper 'On the Probable Error of a Mean' was mainly concerned with inference problems about the mean of a population arising from small samples, Fisher extended 'Student's' method to a wider class of problems (tests of significance for small samples of the difference between two means, and tests concerning coefficients of regression and correlation). Fisher felt that to provide a more unified treatment of these problems, it would be more appropriate to construct tables for $t = z\sqrt{n-1}$ instead of z. This transition from z to t (the letter t presumably being suggested by 'Student') came about through Fisher's desire to deal with the concept of 'degrees of freedom' and occurred in about 1922 (Eisenhart, 1979). This distribution has been known since as 'Student's t Distribution', and it is undoubtedly one of the most frequently used tools of the statistician. The Society of Actuaries in Ireland proudly displays a 't' in its crest in recognition of its importance in actuarial science and its 'Irish significance'. R. A. Fisher wrote of 'Student' in 1939:

> How did it come about that a man of Student's interests and training should have made an advance of fundamental mathematical importance, the possibility of which had been overlooked by the very brilliant mathematicians who have studied the theory of errors? . . . One immense advantage which Student possessed was his concern with and respon-sibility for, the practical interpretation of experimental data. If more mathematicians shared this advantage there can be no doubt that mathematical research would be more fruitfully directed than it often is.

The distribution of the sample correlation coefficient was a problem of considerable practical importance with which Gosset was also very interested. In 1908 he published in *Biometrika* 'The Probable Error of a Correlation Coefficient' where he investigated the probability distribution of the (small) sample correlation coefficient from a bivariate normal distribution. Using the same criminal data as in his 'Probable Error of a Mean' paper, he was able by simulation to 'guess' the appropriate distri-bution (one of Karl Pearson's type II curves) in the situation where there is no correlation. He made some interesting comments about the more general problem (for nonzero correlation) but the actual probability distribution was beyond his grasp. R. A. Fisher elegantly solved the problem in *Biometrika* in 1915, justifying 'Student's' superb insight and intuition.

Guinness, as a large consumer of barley, was very interested in agricultural experimentation. Gosset, with his statistical knowledge, eventually became involved in the design and analysis of such experiments, many of which were carried out under the supervision of the Irish Department of Agriculture. R. A. Fisher is credited with developing in the 1920s the statistical tools of analysis of variance to assist in the planning and interpretation of such experiments, but even Fisher himself on many occasions paid tribute to the pioneering work done in this area (through published work, correspondence and discussion) by 'Student'. Fisher and 'Student' did, however, come into open controversy on the subject of balance versus randomness in experimental design. Fisher was a strong proponent of randomness, but 'Student' was not willing to use a plot arrangement in agricultural design if the resulting arrangement was biased in relation to already known fertility aspects of a field. Although this was an area on which they never agreed, this did not infringe on the tremendous respect they had for each other.

In an era when the postal service was superior to that which we have now and when written communication was important for somewhat isolated scientists, Gosset was an excellent and enthusiastic correspondent with many agriculturists, statisticians and other experimenters. His visit to University College London in 1906 led to an extensive and lifelong correspondence with Karl Pearson, and eventually Pearson's son, Egon. Fisher's letter to Gosset in 1912 on the z distribution also led to a mutually fruitful lifelong correspondence (many of his letters to Fisher are available in Gosset, 1970), even though the strong personalities of Fisher and Karl Pearson led them into considerable controversy on various statistical issues. Gosset was an extremely able but modest man, and he possessed both considerable diplomacy and a keen sense of humour. In later years he attempted to keep the lines of communication open between his old professor, K. Pearson, and Fisher. He was a school-mate of G.H. Hardy, and in a postscript of a letter to Fisher (15 December 1918) he wrote, 'I think you were a pupil of G.H. Hardy and often wonder whether he put you on to my problems. I once sent him an offprint with an appeal for help, but though I used to see a lot of him at school and even while we were undergraduates he did not reply: he always did scorn applied mathematics except cricket averages.'

An excerpt from a letter to Fisher (12 October 1922) gives an indication of the circumstances in Ireland at the time, but which perhaps could have been written at some other periods of Irish history:

You ask whether we are all right through 'the riots'. We don't have 'riots' here although they do in Belfast. Here it is some unobtrusive individual who throws a bomb at a lorry-load of soldiers in a crowded street. He doesn't often damage the soldiers who are mostly driving h for l nor do the soldiers often hit him, but there are others. I've never seen one of their performances myself. The rest of the work is done at night and we are none of us free from the fear of it.

In another letter to Fisher (22 March 1926) he wrote:

I am writing to warn you that when in London last week I met one Dr Neyman who was anxious to visit you and Rothamsted. He is a Pole who has been sent to perfect himself in 'Statistics' by the authorities, agricultural and others, of Warsaw (I think) at the expense of the Rockefeller foundation. He is fonder of algebra than correlation tables and is the only person except yourself that I have heard talk about maximum likelihood as if he enjoyed it.

Dr Jerzy Neyman and Egon Pearson, who often looked to Gosset for guidance, eventually collaborated to establish much of modern day theory of hypothesis testing, such as the Neyman–Pearson Lemma.

Gosset was a man of wide interests and pursued many hobbies in spite of his heavy workload and dedication to Guinness (McMullen, 1970; Cunliffe, 1976). He enjoyed outdoor pursuits, in particular golf, hunting and fishing. He loved to use a pen-knife and was interested in carpentry, building several boats, one of which had a rudder at each end for the particular benefit of fly fishermen and its design was described in the 28 March 1936 issue of *Field*. He was a keen gardener and made some barley crosses in his own garden. In order to accelerate their multiplication (the crosses were known as Student I and II), he had one generation grown in New Zealand – eventually they were discarded as failures. He was a keen fruit grower with a particular interest in apples and pears, and he developed some promising logan-raspberry hybrids in the 1920s, two of which were named 'Jamberry' and 'Paddyberry'.

William Sealy Gosset or 'Student' was indeed a talented and diversified scientist and statistician who was respected by many. R. A. Fisher wrote of 'Student' in 1939, 'His life was one full of fruitful scientific ideas and his versatility extended beyond his interests in research. In spite of his many activities it is the student of Student's test of significance who has won, and deserved to win, a unique place in the history of scientific method.'

Bibliography

Philip J. Boland (1984) 'A biographical glimpse of William Sealy Gosset', *The American Statistician*, **38** (3), pp. 179–83.

Joan Fisher Box (1981) 'Gosset, Fisher and the *t*-distribution', *The American Statistician*, **35**, pp. 61–7.

Denis Conniffe (1990/1991) 'R. A. Fisher and the development of statistics – a view in his centenary year', *Journal of the Statistical and Social Inquiry Society of Ireland*, **XXVI** (iii), pp. 55–108.

Stella Cunliffe (1976) 'Interaction', *Journal of the Royal Statistical Society*, Series A, **139**, pp. 1–19.

Churchill Eisenhart (1979) 'On the transition from Student's *z* to Student's *t*', *The American Statistician*, **33**, pp. 6–10.

R.A. Fisher (1939) 'Student', *Annals of Eugenics*, 1–9.

W. S. Gosset (1970) *Letters from W.S. Gosset to R.A. Fisher, 1915–1936* (with summaries by R.A. Fisher and a foreword by L. McMullen), Dublin: Arthur Guinness, Son & Co. (Dublin) Ltd. Issued for private circulation.

L. McMullen (1970) 'Student as a man', *Studies in the History of Statistics and Probability*, Vol. I, Charles Griffin & Co., 355–60.

E.S. Pearson (1970a) 'Student as statistician', *Studies in the History of Statistics and Probability*, Vol. I, Charles Griffin & Co., pp. 360–403.

E.S. Pearson (1970b) 'Some Early correspondence between W.S. Gosset, R.A. Fisher, and Karl Pearson, with notes and comments', *Studies in the History of Statistics and Probability*, Vol. I, Charles Griffin & Co., pp. 405–17.

R. L. Plackett (ed.) with G. A. Barnard (1990) *'Student' – A Statistical Biography of William Sealy Gosset*, based on writings by E.S. Pearson, Oxford.

Charles Smith (1987) personal communication.

Student (1906) 'On the error of counting with a haemacytometer', *Biometrika*, **4**, pp. 351–60.

Student (1908a) 'The probable error of a mean'. *Biometrika*, **6**, pp. 1–25.

Student (1908b) 'The probable error of a correlation coefficient', *Biometrika*, **7**, pp. 302–10.

15

Walter Heitler 1904–81

L. O'Raifeartaigh
Dublin Institute for Advanced Studies
G. Rasche
University of Zürich

T FIRST SIGHT IT MAY seem strange to find Walter Heitler, who was born and educated in Karlsruhe, Germany, listed among Irish scientists. However, he spent the years 1941–49 at the Dublin Institute for Advanced Studies and shortly after his arrival became an Irish citizen. Although he left the country in 1949 he retained both his citizenship and his links with the country until his death. Indeed his mother and his sister, who taught German at Alexandra College, remained in Ireland until the end of their lives.

Perhaps the most famous of Heitler's contributions to science was the Heitler–London theory of the covalent chemical bond. This theory, which is to be found today in every textbook on chemistry, constituted the final step in explaining the covalent bond in terms of quantum mechanics, and it laid the foundation for the modern theory of organic chemistry. Heitler and Fritz London themselves continued to work in that field only for a relatively short time, but their pioneering work was developed by a host of other workers, including Pauling. What Heitler and London found was that the covalent chemical bond was due to an exchange force that originated in the indistinguishability of identical particles. Thus it had no classical analogue. The simplest example of the covalent bond is provided by the hydrogen molecule, which consists of two atoms, not one. According to the Heitler–London theory this happens because the exchange forces make two H-atoms attract (and repel a third).

Although the chemical bond contribution is the contribution that is best known outside physics, Heitler's contributions within physics were equally profound and much more extensive. Following the work with London, he turned his attention to quantum electrodynamics, in which field he soon became a leading figure. His first major contribution was a formula for electron-position production derived in collaboration with Hans Bethe, who was later awarded the Nobel Prize for his many contributions, including this one. The extension of the formula to arbitrary particle-anti particle production is immediate and is still in use today. A second major contribution was his demonstration (with Homi Bhabha, later director of the Tata Institute, Bombay) that cosmic ray cascades could be explained by quantum electrodynamics alone, without recourse to nuclear forces, as had previously been supposed. As Pascual Jordan, one of the four founders of quantum field theory, remarked in reference to this work:

> It was a great merit of Heitler to have provided by his cascade theory a strong barrier against premature speculations: this allowed the quantum-mechanics of the radiation field to produce a huge harvest of results, before the real conditions for a fundamentally extended theory became visible.

Heitler also worked on nuclear physics at this time, his most important contribution being a celebrated paper on isotopic spin, written in collaboration with Hans Fröhlich and Nikolas Kemmer. This paper extended Heisenberg's theory of isotopic spin from nucleons to mesons, predicted the existence of the neutral pi-meson (which was discovered a decade later) and laid the foundations for the flavour and colour symmetries which are at the heart of the present-day standard models of the non-gravitational interactions. A later contribution was his theory of radiation damping. In the days before the renormalisation of quantum electrodynamics was introduced, his was the only quantum field theory that could be successfully applied at the phenomenological level and Heitler applied it to the theory of cosmic rays. The importance of the damping theory was appreciated even by the hypercritical Wolfgang Pauli, of the Pauli exclusion principle, who wrote:

> Heitler has given a correspondence scheme . . . by which he can eliminate in a Lorentz invariant manner the divergences occurring in the treatment of scattering processes. This scheme consists in adding a new rule to the already existing formalism of quantum mechanics. He hopes to obtain thus an approximate theory which would have the same relation to a

Walter Heitler

future quantum mechanics that Bohr's quantization of classical orbits had to quantum mechanics.

An unsung contribution (because it does not bear his name) should also be mentioned. This is the so-called Gupta–Bleuler mechanism, which is used to ensure that probabilities in quantum electrodynamics remain positive in spite of the indefiniteness of the Minkowski space–time metric. This mechanism is the forerunner of the celebrated Higgs and BRST mechanisms used in today's fundamental interaction (non-abelian gauge) theories. That Heitler was the guiding spirit behind the mechanism can be seen from the fact that Gupta was one of his last post-doctoral fellows in Dublin and Bleuler one of his first in Zürich.

Heitler was not only active in research but was the author of a number of well-known books. His first, called *The Quantum Theory of Radiation*, was first published in 1936 and soon became a standard textbook on Quantum Electrodynamics. Indeed it was the only comprehensive book on the subject until the mid-1950s, with new editions in 1944 and 1954 and five later reprints, the latest being a Dover reprint in 1984. While in Dublin he published a small but delightful monograph on quantum mechanics which has been of great benefit to both physicists and chemists. Later on he published a book on natural philosophy.

Heitler was born in Karlsruhe on 2 January 1904. After normal schooling he began his studies at the Karlsruhe Technische Hochschule, but, feeling that the instruction there did not adequately cover the subjects in which he was interested, he persuaded his father in 1926 to send him to Berlin, where there was a galaxy of star physicists, including Einstein, Planck and von Laue. He learned a great deal of physics in Berlin, but, realising that he would not get any help in obtaining a doctorate, he moved one year later to Munich, where he worked with Arnold Sommerfeld and Karl Herzfeld, obtaining his doctorate (on concentrated chemical solutions) with the latter. On his completion of the doctorate, Sommerfeld obtained for him a Rockefeller fellowship to visit Copenhagen, with the aim of continuing his work on ions in solution. But the quantum mechanics of Heisenberg and Schrödinger had just appeared and, realising its importance, Heitler requested that his fellowship be changed to allow him to work with Schrödinger in Zürich. The request was granted and he arrived there in 1926. In Zürich he had much interaction with Schrödinger, but no direct collaboration. However, it was there that he met London and formulated the theory of the chemical bond. This was at the early age of 23, and had the practical result that Max Born, later Nobel Laureate, immediately offered him an assistantship in Göttingen, which he took up in 1928. His program in Göttingen was to study group theory in relation to quantum mechanics and he took advantage of it to study profoundly all the available works on quantum mechanics and quantum field theory, especially those of Heisenberg, Dirac and Born himself. During his second year at Göttingen Heitler and Gerhard Herzberg were the victims in one of the many 'missed opportunities' in physics, as follows: Their analysis of the bandspectrum of nitrogen in 1929 showed that the ^{14}N nucleus obeyed Bose rather than Fermi statistics. This implied that the neutron was a Fermi particle, and hence could not be a composite of a proton and electron, as was generally supposed. But in the late 1920s, physicists were extremely reluctant to propose the existence of new particles (recall Pauli's hesitation concerning the neutrino and Dirac's identification of the charge-conjugate of the electron with the proton) and in this climate Heitler and Herzberg did not dare follow their result to its logical conclusion, namely the prediction of the neutron as an elementary particle in its own right. As he has said himself: 'Later Herzberg and I were very angry when we realized that we could have predicted the existence of the neutron long before it was discovered experimentally by Chadwick in 1932.'

In spite of the missed opportunity Heitler made good use of his time in Göttingen, where he became Privatdozent in 1929 and developed into a world expert on quantum electrodynamics. These were happy times for him, but as both his parents were Jewish and the National Socialists were beginning to emerge, there was always the possibility of his position at the University being terminated. Because of this he made an extended visit to Moscow to see whether, in that event, he could take refuge there. But he was rather disappointed with the conditions in Russia and returned to Göttingen. When the National Socialists did come to power in 1933, Heitler and others (including Lothar Nordheim and 1962 Nobel-laureat Eugene Wigner) received the expected letters of dismissal. Luckily there existed at the time an arrangement that permitted young physicists at Göttingen to spend a year at Bristol, and Born arranged for Heitler to avail himself of that scheme. At the end of his year in Bristol he was offered a position, though not a permanent one.

Sir Neville Mott had just been appointed professor at Bristol and Heitler was able to interact not only with him but with a number of well-known visitors, such as Bhabha, with whom he collaborated on the cascade theory, and other refugees such as Bethe, Kemmer and Fröhlich, with whom he collaborated on a variety of topics. The famous experimental cosmic ray group of Powell and Blackett was already in operation in Bristol so Heitler was also able to keep in close touch with experiment. It was during his time in Bristol that Heitler published most of his work on quantum electrodynamics and his early work on cosmic rays. When the war broke out in 1939, he was interned on the Isle of Man, along with six of his colleagues from Bristol, including his brother Hans. He was released after some time and returned to Bristol. At this time physicists were being recruited to work on the atomic bomb project but Heitler (along with Kemmer and Fröhlich) declined to take part, a decision which later caused a certain rift between himself and those who participated in the project. Shortly after his return to Bristol he received from Schrödinger an offer of a permanent position at the recently created Dublin Institute for Advanced Studies. Being attracted by the offer, and being advised that, as a German, he might have difficulty in obtaining a permanent position in England, he accepted. At this time he was engaged to Kathleen Nicholson, a research worker in biological science whom he had met in Bristol, and they married shortly after his arrival in Dublin. Their son Eric was born there in 1946.

During his Dublin years Heitler elaborated on his earlier work with Fröhlich and Kemmer, giving for the first time the relations between the cross-sections due to charge-independence (isospin-invariance). But his most important scientific contribution during his Dublin years was the theory of radiation damping. His research was concerned mainly with the application of this theory and quantum electrodynamics in general to cosmic ray physics, which at the time (before the advent of the big accelerators) was the physicists' only access to high energies. Indeed, Heitler and Schrödinger considered the area of cosmic ray physics so important that they urged Eamon de Valera, then Taoiseach, to add a School of Cosmic Physics to the Institute for Advanced Studies. This was done in 1947, and the School incorporated also departments of Astrophysics and Geophysics. During his time in Dublin Heitler collaborated both with the experimental physicists associated with the School of Cosmic Physics, such as Ernest Walton, Ireland's only Nobel laureate in physics, Lanos Janossy, who caused some controversy when he returned to his native Hungary, Thomas Nevin of University College and Cormac O'Ceallaigh of the Cosmic School, both of whom had been members of Powell's group in Bristol. He had, of course, also a close collaboration with many young local theoreticians, such as Jim Hamilton, James McConnell, Sheila Tinney (*née* Power) and Phillip Gormley, and had a sequence of foreign post-doctoral fellows, many of whom, such as Walter Thirring, H. W. Peng, Cecile de Witt (*née* Morette) and Suraj Gupta, have since become international names in their own right. An interesting view of Heitler's impact on the Dublin scene is given by Sir Neville Mott in his Royal Society obituary:

> Heitler is remembered in Dublin for the clarity and interest of his lectures; he was always courteous and very helpful to his students. His influence was largely responsible for the modernisation of university courses in Dublin in theoretical physics, and for the establishment of theoretical and experimental research groups which are still functioning today. For the benefit of chemists he gave an introductory course on wave-mechanics and its application to the theory of the chemical bond. This was published as a small book by the Oxford University Press and must have served as the introduction to wave-mechanism for many of the less mathematically equipped among those who needed the subject.

Heitler visited the United States soon after the war but was less impressed both with the physics and the general environment than he had been on an earlier, pre-war, visit. He was Director of the School of Theoretical Physics at the Dublin Institute for Advanced Studies from 1946 until 1949, when he accepted an invitation to become Professor of Theoretical Physics at the University of Zürich. He had hesitated before accepting the position, as he had been happy in Dublin and appreciated living close to the sea. But in the end the prestige of the Zürich position, whose predecessors included Einstein, von Laue, Debye and Schrödinger, the opportunity to revisit the scene of his earlier successes, the lure of a German-speaking environment and the opportunity to mountain-climb and ski (at both of which he was very proficient) proved irresistible, and he accepted the offer. In spite of many subsequent invitations, he remained in Zürich for the rest of his life. His most successful work in the 1950s, carried out in collaboration with Edmond Arnous from the Institut Henri Poincaré in Paris, was concerned with the natural breadth of spectral lines. He also produced an important paper on detailed balance (which was actually the completion of a note in 1925 on Einstein's derivation of the Planck radiation law). However, he found himself rather out of sympathy with the renormalisation program of quantum electro-dynamics. Although renormalisation made the predictions of the theory completely reliable, and these agreed with the experiments to an uncanny degree of accuracy, Heitler considered it to be merely a clever mathematical addendum to an already existing physical theory, and was concerned by the fact that it evaded the problems posed by the mass-differences of the elementary particles (in particular the proton-neutron mass difference). He tried rather unsuccessfully to remedy this defect in the program using a modified version of his earlier damping theory, and indeed his last public contribution to physics was a talk on the subject at the 1962 Solvay Conference. However, his analysis of the problem was correct in the sense that, although the mass-difference problem is now formulated at the quark, rather than the hadronic, level, it remains unsolved.

Heitler had always a deep interest in philosophy and religion, and from the beginning of the 1960s he began to concentrate more on these subjects. He had no difficulties with physics as such and freely acknowledged the great successes of reductionist science since the time of Galileo. Nor did the advent of quantum mechanics cause him any problem. From his time in Göttingen he had accepted the Born (now called the Copenhagen) interpretation of quantum mechanics, and he had little interest in the objections of Einstein and Schrödinger or in the alternative explanations offered by Louis de Broglie, David Bohm and others. However, he felt that, in spite of its great successes, reductionist science would prove incapable of explaining a variety of aspects of nature, particularly the qualitative and non-local aspects. His opinion was that in many processes, such as biology and evolution, forces other than the known quantitative ones must be at work and that there must exist teleological and non-local laws yet to be discovered.

These thoughts were first formulated in a book which was translated into English in 1961 under the title *Man and Science*. The book proved to be very popular and has been translated into many languages. Afterwards, Heitler elaborated his ideas in a series of articles, and received invitations to lecture on the subject from universities all over Europe. As he once wryly remarked, 'he was now visiting the Philosophical and Theological Departments of Universities where he had once visited the Physics Departments'. He had always had an interest in the anthroposophy of Rudolf Steiner without accepting it fully and towards the end of his life he became a Christian. He died on 15 November 1981.

Heitler received many honours. He was elected a Member of the Royal Irish Academy in 1943, a Member of the Norwegian Royal Society in 1974, a Fellow of the Royal Society in 1948 and received honorary doctorates from both Dublin universities. He was awarded the Max Planck Medal of the German Physical Society in 1968. In 1970 he became one of the few physicists to receive the Marcel Benoist prize, and in 1979 he was awarded the Gold Medal of the Humboldt Society.

16

David Robert Bates 1916–94

Derrick Crothers

The Queen's University of Belfast

D AVID ROBERT BATES WAS born in Omagh. He and his sister attended a one-room-one-teacher school: 'Miss Quigley's'. In 1925 the family moved to Belfast; Bates attended the Royal Belfast Academical Institution and developed a love of science and mathematics, building a small chemistry laboratory at home.

In 1934 Bates entered the Queen's University of Belfast (QUB) Science Faculty and studied chemistry and pure mathematics. However, he took a First in 1937 in Experimental and Mathematical Physics, inspired by George Emeleus and Harrie Massey. An MSc (with J. J. Unwin) on Recombination in the Upper Atmosphere followed in 1938.

In 1939 Massey was appointed to the Goldsmidt Chair of Mathematics at University College London (UCL). Bates followed. However, war arrived. UCL was closed and they were assigned to the Admiralty Research Laboratory, Teddington. Menacing aircraft-laid mines could be activated by a ship's magnetic field. Bates took on measurements on scaled ship-models to reduce magnetic fields via current-carrying coils. In 1941 Massey was appointed Deputy Chief Scientist in the Mine Design Department and took with him Gunn, Crick and Buckingham. Bates made his mark as Chairman of the Mechanical-Engineering Committee and Massey later wrote 'he introduced a breath of fresh air into a moribund subject of great importance for the defence effort'.

With war ending in 1945, Massey and Bates returned to UCL and wrote major papers which quantitatively transformed the study of the ionised regions of the Earth's atmosphere. Bates investigated the physics of luminosity of the atmosphere and predicted that if sodium were released at 90km altitudes a spectacular yellow glow would appear at twilight. The successful experiment was an important stimulus to the UK Space Research programme. He and Nicolet worked on many chemical species including atmospheric methane, water vapour and ozone.

Bates returned to QUB in 1951 to take the Chair in Applied Mathematics (from 1968: Theoretical Physics). He built up an internationally renowned School, now the Theoretical and Computational Physics Research Division (TCPRD), making monumental contributions to theoretical atomic, molecular and atmospheric physics.

Many postgraduate research students, postdoctoral research assistants and visiting scientists passed through the Division. All retained an abiding and affectionate regard for Sir David and Lady Bates. In December 1992, Physics at QUB gained a top grading in the UK universities research-assessment exercise. This gave David much pleasure.

Loyal to Queen's and Northern Ireland, Bates took a deep interest in the 'troubles'. He was aware of paramilitary violence and dusk-to-dawn curfews. Unsurprisingly Bates was a founder member of APNI (Alliance Party) in 1970, when he wrote an influential article in *The Times*. As APNI Vice-President he was a keen activist, regularly attending the Annual Party Conference. He was delighted that the elected APNI Members of the First Northern Ireland Assembly formed the 1974 Powersharing Executive with the Unionist Party of Northern Ireland and the SDLP. He continued to support APNI non-sectarian policies, abhorring violence. The peace discussions of the late 1990s would have brought deep satisfaction to Bates, as would the 1998 pro-Agreement vote, north and south.

Bates was elected Fellow of the Royal Society in 1955 and Vice-President of the Royal Irish Academy, having been elected a Member in 1952. He was knighted for his services to science in 1978. He was elected a Member of the International Academy of Astronautics in 1961, an Honorary Foreign Member of the American Academy of Arts and Sciences in 1974, an Associate Member of the Royal Academy, Belgium in 1979, a Foreign Associate of the National Academy of Science, USA in 1984 and an Honorary Member of the European Geophysical Union which established a Medal in his name in 1992.

Bates was awarded the Royal Society Hughes Medal in 1971, the Institute of Physics (IOP) Chree Medal in 1973, the Royal Astronomical Society Gold Medal in 1977 and the American Geophysical Union Fleming Medal in 1987. From 2000, the IOP Division of Atomic, Molecular, Optical and Plasma Physics will award annually the Sir David Bates Prize for excellence. QUB, the New University of Ulster, the National University of Ireland, and the Universities of York (Ontario), Dublin, Glasgow and York awarded him Honorary degrees. He was Editor in Chief of *Planetary and Space Science* and of *Advances in Atomic and Molecular Processes* and a Correspondent for *Comments on Atomic and Molecular Physics*.

Bates was an inspirational figure in theoretical physics. Excellent accounts given by Seaton (1996) and by Dalgarno (1997) include his work on atmospheric physics, light-particle collisions, recombination and extra-terrestrial civilisations.

Bates was mostly occupied [257]* during his latter years with heavy-particle collisions and recombination: 'he should have left time to talk at some length on both of these; having not done so, he preferred to say nothing about them rather than risk the distortion that high selectivity might bring'. His immense contributions to heavy-particle (ions, atoms, molecules) collision theory are reviewed below for the period 1951 to 1989, during which a principal motivation was upper-atmosphere physics.

Returning to QUB, and reducing the risk of duplication, Bates (and Massey) agreed that electron-collisions should be the prerogative of the UCL group and heavy-particle-collisions that of the embryo Belfast group of Alex Dalgarno, Benno Moiseiwitsch and Alan Stewart. He 'was trebly blessed in the membership of that group'[257]. A prescient inception! Bates collaborated with many other physicists, including Mike Seaton, Sydney Chapman, Lyman Spitzer, Fred Hoyle, R. A. Buckingham, John Lewis, Jim Boyd, Ron McCarroll, Coulter McDowell, Glen Bates, Ed Zipf, Alan Williams, Marcel Nicolet, Tom Patterson, Jack Smith, David Williams, Roy Moffett, Ray Flannery, Arthur Kingston, Kenneth Bell, Anthony Holt, Derrick Crothers, Alan Hibbert, Robin McDonough and Richard Tweed.

The embryo group embarked on potential-energy curve-crossing X I – IV ([68], Dalgarno 1954, [74], [84]), fast collisions Y I – VII ([57], [66], Moiseiwitsch and Stewart 1954, [73], Boyd et al. 1957, Adler and Moiseiwitsch 1957, [87]) and electron capture Z I – III

---

* The references [.], refer to Bates's bibliography, a photocopy of which is available from the Royal Society London Library (Dalgarno, 1997).

([51], Dalgarno and Yadav 1953, [58]). Bates reviewed the period methodically [83], [111], [118], [146], [165], [164], [171], [174], [180], [211], [245], [257], [272], and [304].

Bates and Dalgarno [83] reviewed their work [51], [52], [57], [58], [63], [66], [68], [73], [74], [76] and [82] and described [51] charge transfer in p-H collisions in the first-Born wave treatment. This intuitive work is consistent with the 'boundary-corrected Born' treatment. They acknowledged [51,52] Mott and Massey (1949). Bates et al. [52] posed the perturbed stationary-state (PSS) treatment of ion-atom collisions at low impact energies. Describing the relative nuclear motion quantally, they solved the coupled equations using a partial-wave analysis. They applied a Wentzel–Kramers–Brillouin (WKB) semiclassical distortion approximation with Jeffreys' (J) connection formula at the larger classical turning point, enforcing causality. They studied symmetric resonance using an impact-parameter treatment for σ – σ and σ – π transitions.

Bates and Griffing [Y I:57] used the Born approximation for excitation and ionization in p-H and H-H collisions. Bates and Dalgarno [Z III:58] studied fast p capturing e^- from H(1s) to form H(n), $n \leq 4$. Bates and Massey [63] considered excitation, charge-transfer, ionization and detachment in slow collisions. They wanted to explain the highly intense luminosity of meteors passing through the earth's atmosphere. A dynamical molecular non-adiabatic treatment was required in the 1932 spirit of Landau, Zener and Stueckelberg (LZS). Excitation in O-Fe collisions was much more likely than in H-He collisions, due to the large number of excited Fe states. Charge-transfer probabilities can be large owing to a long-range curve-crossing or a constant resonance-defect. For ionization and detachment, autoionization of the quasi-molecule in atom-atom collisions at small separations is likely.

Bates and Griffing [Y II:66] applied the Born approximation to

$$H(1s) + H(1s) \rightarrow H(2l) + H(\Sigma). \qquad (1)$$

Bates and Moiseiwitsch [X I:68] applied LZS to capture in Be^{++}, Si^{++} and Mg^{++} +H. They calculated rate coefficients for Coulomb, inverse-cube and polarizability potentials. Bates and Griffing [Y IV:73] extended Y II to the products H(3l) + H(3l) or H(3l ; Σ) + H^+ +e^-. Double transitions were insignificant. Bates, studying recombination in the atmospheric F layers, considered ion-molecule collisions [76] involving charge-transfer or ion-atom interchange. Charge-transfer was unlikely but reactive ion-atom exchange would be significant producing much higher mean energies in the molecular ion. Bates and Lewis [X III:74] considered transfer from H^- to p

Sir David Bates. Portrait by Basil Blackshaw.

to form H (n), with n ≤ 3 and found that n = 2 dominated at higher energies but n = 3 at the lower. Bates studied the primary auroral stream [82] and H, He and Na excited-state lines of emission [83].

Bates gave an account of transitions [111] in heavy-particle collisions. He outlined the first- and second-Born impact-parameter and wave treatments using *travelling* atomic and molecular orbitals and Bates–McCarroll longitudinal [179] electron-translation-factors (ETFs) [95]. Bates [111] outlined the $P(1-P) + (1-P)P = 2P(1-P)$ LZ phase-averaged impact-parameter probability for a non-adiabatic collision with two passages of the curve-crossing: transition followed by no transition or vice versa. Bates [108] noted that LZ theory was restricted to σ – σ transitions at sufficiently low velocities.

Bates [118] reviews Born wave and impact-parameter treatments, including Coulomb [119], [124] and straight-line trajectories. Excitation, ionization, capture and hybrid events are discussed. Both *travelling* atomic- [97] and molecular- [95] orbital expansions are considered with classical ETFs included [122]. The effect of distortion is emphasised [99], [110], [116]. The problems with the perturbed, rotating-atom (PRA) approximation are outlined [93], [98]. Bates's physical intuition told him that the PRA approximation cannot be correct since at small impact-parameters the electronic cloud of a p-orbital cannot keep up with the rapidly rotating, internuclear axis. Bates and D. Williams rectified this [133] by including 2pσ – 2pπ rotational coupling. Bates and A. Williams [Y VII:87] replaced the H target [66] by He. They calculated electron loss from the projectile, while excitation of He $(1s2p^1P)$ or elastic scattering were dominant simultaneous processes.

Bates and Lynn [100] demonstrated that accidental resonance results in small cross-sections for

$$He^{++} + H(1s) \rightarrow He^+(n = 2) + H^+$$
$$H^+ + O(^3P) \rightarrow H(1s) + O^+ (^4S)$$
$$O^+(^2D) + N_2(X^1\Sigma_g^+ \, v = 0) \rightarrow O(^3P) + N_2^+(A^2\Pi_u \, v = 1).$$

The impact-parameter 'refined orthogonal treatment' is presented [118, 122] for travelling molecular and atomic orbitals, exhibiting Galilean invariance, gauge invariance and detailed balancing. Bates and McCarroll [122] showed that in p-H collisions, 3^0 capture probabilities are sensitive to molecular ETFs, notably the Stueckelberg phase. They discuss dominant radiative charge-transfer at thermal and relativistic impact-energies. Bates [118] records [123] the failure of the 1932 treatment of Stueckelberg for non-crossing transitions.

Bates [164] returned to the PSS approximation [52] and travelling, molecular orbitals with rotating-reference frame [95, 122, 133]. The H_2^+ correlation diagram [154] indicates that many molecular energy-levels make truncation of the PSS set contentious. His experience [93, 94, 98] was that *all* allowed azimuthal and magnetic degeneracies must be included. He reviews [171] the mutual neutralization of positive and negative ions including $H^+ + H^-$ [84] and Be^+, $Mg^+ + H^+$ [135] avoided crossings. He gives the rate coefficient via the L-Z probability $2P(1 - P)$. The effects of any ambient gas were evaluated [228, 244]. For Mg^+, LZ is found to be infinitesimal [135]. Bates and Reid [168] considered $H^+ + H(n) \rightarrow H(n) + H^+$ at low energies, to compare total cross-section scaling (n^3) in contrast with classical estimates (n^4). Bates [211, §3] discusses the Massey criterion for an effective cross-section, namely

$$\text{Min } (l \, \Delta E/\hbar v) >> 1 \qquad (2)$$

where v is the impact velocity, ΔE the potential-energy jump in the non-adiabatic domain, $\hbar$ Planck's reduced constant and l the width of the domain. Criterion (2) is based on LZS and RZ. Bates gives an elaborate discussion of sequential mechanisms [208] for the ionization of Na in flames, listing his other quantal work [257]. He applies [128, 194] the impact-parameter treatment to the quantal processes, p-H excitation and ionization and the wave treatment [142] to impact ionization of Na. With Crothers, he applies [149] the wave treatment to the three-electron collision of H with He. Fair agreement with experiment was obtained for the $1\,^1S - 3\,^3P$ He transition.

Bates and Kingston reviewed work in which nuclei *and* electrons are treated classically: capture [140], detachment [151] and excitation, ionization and electron loss [166]. Bates [174, 211] reviews classical Thomas-double-scattering in ion-molecule [129] and ion-atom [144] rearrangement collisions with quantal target-electron velocity distributions [151]. Bates with Snyder [188] and G. Bates [206] improved the classical binary-encounter descriptions of p-H capture and ionization using a classical finite characteristic collision-time. A perceptive remark [211] concerns Wannier applying classical mechanics to a quantal phenomenon, threshold ionization with two electrons leaving, with equal and opposite velocities. Bates and Reid [167] refine the classical treatment of p-H [144] by matching the three motion-constants to their quantal analogues; the classical and quantal binary-encounter models are contrasted [172, 182].

Semiclassically [180] a wave-number

$$k(R) = M\, v(R)/\hbar \qquad (3)$$

is large, where M is the heavy-particle reduced mass and v (R) the radial velocity. The classical action is of order $1/\hbar$ and the quantal corrections of order $\hbar^n$ ($n \geq 0$). This is not the impact-parameter treatment. Bates and Holt [146] address the 3-D JWKB atomic and molecular expansions. The first-Born model semi-classical atomic-expansion mimics the quantal expansion better than the impact-parameter one. Bates and Crothers [165] constructed the 1D JWKB atomic treatment, the coupled differential equations per partial wave reducing to impact-parameter equations by forcing a common classical turning-point. Causality replaces acausality. A distorted-wave Coulomb model was solved exactly and semiclassically. Excellent agreement was obtained at 0.85eV above threshold (3.4eV). Bates and Sprevak [173, 178] applied this 1D treatment to large-angle scattering in p-H collisions.

Bates [211, §4] reviews *exothermic* ion-molecule reactions, observing that (2) may not necessarily imply *low* charge-transfer cross-sections for

$$O^+ + O_2 \rightarrow O + O_2^+ + 1.5eV \qquad (4)$$

of importance in recombination in the atmospheric F layers. Bates and Nicolet [107, 115] considered ion-atom exchanges

$$O^+ + N_2 \rightarrow NO^+ + N + 1.1eV$$
$$O^+ + O_2 \rightarrow O_2^+ + O + 1.5eV \qquad (5)$$

which were much slower than supposed: otherwise all the O^+ ions would disappear within a few seconds of sunset, contrary to observation. Many chemical reactions *are* quicker than LZS predictions due to the higher number of dimensions of ion-atom exchange, and are important in analysing planetary ionospheres and interstellar clouds.

Bates reviews [245, 86] the airglow (nightglow, dayglow and twilight) and auroras and discusses [218] the $^2D_{3/2,5/2} \rightarrow {}^4S_{3/2}$ green doublet of N at 5198-5201Å, the $^1D_2 \rightarrow {}^3P_{2,1}$ red doublet of O at 6300-6364Å, the $^1S_0 \rightarrow {}^1D_2$ auroral green light [243] of O at 5577Å, the $^1S_0 \rightarrow {}^3P_1$ ultraviolet line of O at 2972 Å and the $^2P \rightarrow D_{1,2}$ sodium doublet at 5896 and 5890Å [245].

Bates [163] considers reactions in the D to F ionosphere-layers. Transitions may be electronic or chemical involving O, N, C, H and He atoms in ionic or molecular form, including mutual neutralization, associative detachment, ion-atom exchange, charge-transfer, dissociative charge-transfer, Penning detachment and molecule exchange. Bates [85] discusses the composition and structure of the atmosphere, and uses LZS [306] to calculate rate coefficients for

$$N(^2P) + O(^3P) \rightarrow N(^2D) + O(^3P)$$
$$N(^2D) + O^+(^4S) \rightarrow N^+(^2P) + O(^3P)$$
$$N^+(^3P) + O(^3P) \rightarrow N(^4S) + O^+(^4S),$$

in reasonable accord with aeronomers' estimates. Bates and Hibbert [239] consider the mystery auroral feature at λ 2145Å.

Bates with Holt [141] and Reid [162] describes

$$H^+ + H_2^+ (150, v, J) \rightarrow H^+ + H^+ + H (\Sigma)$$

using the first-Born approximation with a Cohen-Coulson H_2^+ wavefunction, and

$$H_2^+ + H_2 \rightarrow \quad H_2^+ (v') + H_2 (v'')$$
$$H_2 (v'') + H_2^+ (v').$$

A series [192, 214, 224, 234, 265, 266, 269] on ion-molecule association is reviewed [272]. Another on ion-molecule collisions includes Langevin scattering and dipole and quadrapole adiabatic-invariance treatment of hitting collisions [216, 241, 252, 268, 273, 286, 304 §2].

David Bates was one of the greatest twentieth-century Irish scientists. He was a brilliant, innovative and productive theoretical physicist and chemist. He was a very modest, kind and generous person, an inspiration to generations of students. After his retirement in 1982, QUB named the building which houses the Theoretical and Computational Physics Research Division, the David Bates Building. He was especially proud of 'having his name over the shop' and continued to work in his office, stimulating everyone by his perceptive questions. He was a most devoted husband to Barbara and loving father to their two children Katharine and Adam. The Queen's University of Belfast, Northern Ireland and science have lost a man of immense distinction who will be long remembered.

Acknowledgements

I am very grateful to Lady Bates and Dr D. Sprevak for their very kind, helpful assistance and to Professor A. Dalgarno, MRIA FRS, and Professor M. J. Seaton, FRS, for reprints of Dalgarno (1997) and Seaton (1996).

Bibliography

J. Adler and B. L. Moiseiwitsch (1957) *Proceedings Physical Society A*, **70**, p. 117

J. Boyd, B. L. Moiseiwitsch and A. L. Stewart (1957) *Proceedings Physical Society A*, **70**, p. 110

A. Dalgarno (1954) *Proceedings Physical Society A*, **67**, p. 1010

A. Dalgarno (1997) *Biogr. Mem. Fellows Royal Society*. London, **43**, 47.

A. Dalgarno and H. N. Yadav (1953) *Proceedings Physical Society A*, **66**, p. 173

B. L. Moiseiwitsch and A. L. Stewart (1954) *Proceedings Physical Society A*, **67**, p. 1069

N. F. Mott and H. S. W. Massey (1933, 1949, 1965) *The Theory of Atomic Collisions*, Oxford (1st, 2nd, 3rd editions)

M. J. Seaton (1996) *Quarterly Journal of the Royal Astronomical Society*, **37**, p. 81.

17

Andrew Young 1919–92

Gerald Peter Shannon
University of Ulster, Coleraine

ALTHOUGH NOT AN IRISHMAN, nor having any discernible Irish ancestry, Andrew Young spent the last third of his lifetime in Ireland where he made many contributions to its mathematical community. He published in many areas of applied mathematics during his professional career, which was spent first at the University of Liverpool and then the New University of Ulster, until the latter merged with the Ulster Polytechnic. In 1983, Andrew retired early at the age of 63, prior to the merger in 1984, in order to make room for new blood.

Andrew Young was born on 16 December, 1919, in Edentown, Lancashire. His parents were Andrew Young, a foreman railway joiner, and Ruth Nicholson Young (*née* Peill). Andrew was the seventh son of that name in his family, but not all so named were eldest sons. The Youngs and the Peills were both families of artisans, the former from the Lanark/Carluke region of Scotland and the latter from Ambleside/Keswick in Cumbria. The family was a large one of six girls and five boys, which eventually settled in Carlisle. Only one of Andrew's ancestors showed any academic bent, namely his paternal uncle, David, who was a graduate of Glasgow University.

Andrew's education started at Stanwix Council School, from which his two surviving reports give a glimpse of the future scholar with a broad range of interests. In Standard V (age 10) he came second in a class of 45 gaining 19.5/20 for English, 17/20 Composition, 20/20 Spelling,

14/20 Handwriting (!), 47/50 Arithmetic & Mensuration, 19/20 History and 20/20 Homework. This list is incomplete but fully representative. Next year in Standard VI he came first out of 26 with similar marks. However, his Arithmetic was 'marred occasionally by carelessness' – the sign of an over-active mind perhaps. Following Stanwix, having won a scholarship, he moved up to Carlisle Grammar School where his progress was of a very high standard across the board, yet, once again, we come across reports of 'liable to carelessness' – a trait which was to amuse and sometimes infuriate future colleagues.

Before discussing Andrew's career at grammar school and university, we shall pause to consider the financial difficulties he and his family faced in the grim economic climate of the early 1930s. Full-time secondary education was a luxury then, and Andrew needed to support himself and his siblings. To do so he would rise early each morning to milk cows, lay hedges and generally help out on a local farm. He then walked several miles to start school. It was during these years that he became an expert at that quintessentially Cumbrian art of fell running, which included hunting foxes on foot. Yet despite it all, he coped most successfully with a demanding curriculum.

At Carlisle Grammar School he was a first-rate all-round student, showing particular excellence in mathematics and physics, yet playing a full part in extra-mural activities (dramatics, debating and chess). He was always placed in the top five out of *c.* thirty, with one exception when he came sixth. In 1936 he entered form Va and became a pupil of the Cambridge Wrangler, G. C. Archer.

From then on Archer was Andrew's teacher of mathematics and mechanics (a certain C. S. J. taking him for physics). In 1938, as a result of Archer's constant inspiration and encouragement, Andrew won a Harkness Scholarship (the highest award open to competition among entrant students) to enter United College and St Mary's College of the University, St Andrews. He quickly made his mark, winning the Carstairs Prize for Mathematics in 1939 and the Miller Prize for Mathematics in 1940. Mathematics at St Andrew's was very strong in those days with H. W. Turnbull as Professor and lecturers of the calibre of D. E Rutherford and C.A. Coulson. As can now be imagined, Andrew did not let mathematics dominate his life. He took time off to take part in the Kate Kennedy Club (when he was a bejant), to found the University's Cross Country Club, to be elected to the Students' Representative Council, and to hold the offices of Captain of the Athletic Team and President of the

Mathematical and Physical Society. He was also a sergeant in the Officers' Training Corps.

All of that had happened by 1940, when he married Elizabeth Agnes Justice Christie (1922–79), a bookkeeper, was awarded his Ordinary degree in Mathematics and Physics and was called up for the war. His war service ran from 20 December 1940 until 6 January 1946 as a combatant officer in the Border Regiment. After an initial posting to India in July 1941 (two days after registering the birth of his first daughter, Veronica), he was subsequently wounded by shrapnel in both arm and scrotum at the battle of Kohima. This took him back to India and out of combat for the remainder of the war – a war that converted him to pacifism and membership of the Society of Friends. After demobilisation he returned to St Andrew's to continue his studies and to see, after so long, Elsa and Veronica. He took his First in Applied Mathematics in June 1947. True to form, he played the rôle of Napier of Merchiston in the Kate Kennedy Club procession of 1946. After a brief spell as an actuary with a Manchester insurance firm, Andrew started his academic career as a Lecturer in Applied Mathematics at Liverpool University in 1948, the year his second daughter, Wendy, was born.

At Liverpool, where Professor L. Rosenhead was a demanding head of department, Andrew progressed steadily through the ranks:

1958 Senior Lecturer in Applied Mathematics
1959 Senior Lecturer in Numerical Analysis and Director of the Computer Laboratory 1961 Reader in Numerical Analysis
1965 Professor of Numerical Analysis
1966 Head of Department of Computational and Statistical Science

Professor Rosenhead was very keen that his staff should hold doctorates, but at first Andrew had no idea for a thesis topic. Eventually he decided on the numerical analysis of the irregular motions of the earth's axis. This was to be the first period of his life in mathematical research. The other three periods covered biomathematics, numerical analysis and operational research. In all Andrew published eight papers in geophysics, eighteen in numerical analysis, seven in biomathematics and eight in operational research.

His PhD on 'The Rotation of the Earth's Axis' was awarded by Liverpool University in 1959. It was based on an essay explaining the import of his eight papers on the topic. These brought him into collaboration with Sir Harold Jeffreys and invitations to speak at major international conferences.

Andrew Young, *c.* 1960

He was elected a Fellow of the Royal Astronomical Society on 11 May 1951 and granted free fellowship in 1985.

Here is a catalogue of his geophysical activities:

1954 participation on the International Solar Eclipse Expedition in Sweden as an adviser on the numerical problems concerning data reduction;

1955 Leverhulme Research award to visit astronomers studying variation of latitude in Italy, Sardinia and Belgium; 1958 invitation to Xth General Assembly of the International Astronomical Union, Moscow;

1960 invited address on the Future of the International Latitude Service, Helsinki;

1961 elected a member of IAU and appointed to Commission XII (Variation of Latitude).

It is worthy of note that these investigations were undertaken before high powered computers were generally available, and that Andrew's philosophy and methodology were highly inter-disciplinary, blending the intuition of the scientist with the rigour of the mathematician.

During this period Andrew was instrumental in obtaining Liverpool University's first computer. The machine was purchased without the benefit of external financial support and for four years, until the original machine was replaced, he made it pay its way by obtaining industrial contracts to solve management problems.

Before the completion of his work on geophysics, Andrew had started to supervise research students in all the other areas mentioned above. In all he had 32 successful PhD students and about seven MSc students. He was most conscientious in his duties, making sure that his students received regular supervisions on clearly defined and manageable problems. All his MScs and eleven PhDs were from Liverpool, the remainder graduated from the New University of Ulster at Coleraine. This impressive output is even more remarkable given the unusually large number who are now professors of mathematics throughout the world. In 1968 Andrew was appointed first Professor of Mathematics at Coleraine and began his remarkable training of overseas mathematicians. Most of these came from Greece where the majority are now mathematics professors. On top of his professorial duties he served a spell as Dean of the School of Physical Sciences and was a member of Senate, Council and Court.

During the Coleraine years his numerical analysis research consisted of applications of linear programming to industrial problems, numerical procedures for approximation by spline functions and approximation in the Chebyshev and L^1 norms.

He continued the biomathematical work started at Liverpool on population dynamics, the simulation of the liver on a computer and effective means of determining total lung capacity. These applications of mathematics to medicine resulted in his appointment to the editorial board of *Thorax* in 1964.

It was the investigation of manpower planning problems in the British university system that initiated Andrew's work in operational research. His first paper with Almond provided the foundation stone of the modern theory of non-homogeneous Markov chain models in data analysis, and with P-C. G. Vassiliou and T. Abodunde (at Coleraine) he continued applying these ideas to non-linear models for the promotion and recruitment of staff.

On top of his academic publications Andrew published reports for the Nursing Council and Association of University Teachers, together with popular articles for *The Education Times* and the *New Scientist*.

It is now time to consider Andrew's extra-mural activities. As well as his fellowship of the Royal Astronomical Society, he was a Fellow of the British Computer Society and a founder Fellow of the Institute of Mathematics and its Applications. He served on the council of the latter, and took great delight in regaling his colleagues with accounts of a council meeting chaired by Prince Philip at Buckingham Palace.

Always a highly political animal, Andrew was deeply involved with the Association of University Teachers, in Liverpool he was a Labour councillor sitting on the City's Education Finance Committee and in Northern Ireland he was a dedicated member of the Abercorn Trust (for which he raised £7,000 by completing the 500 miles of the Ulster Way) and Christian Aid. He revived the Coleraine Meeting of the Society of Friends, bequeathed his house to them and established the Quaker Peace Education Project (Andrew Young Memorial), University of Ulster, Magee Campus, Co. Londonderry.

In conclusion Andrew was the most generous and convivial of men. In the mid-1960s there was a serious outbreak of foot and mouth disease in Great Britain and horse racing was banned. However, Andrew developed a computer simulation for the sports pages of the *Daily Express*, gaining some useful royalties which he donated to fund prizes for outstanding students of Computer Information Systems and Mathematics with Computer Science at Liverpool University, and Mathematics at the

University of Ulster. Until 1999 the Liverpool foundation was anonymous, but in the summer of that year his daughter, Wendy, presented the first Andrew Young prizes.

He is still warmly remembered in the Senior Common Room for his outrageous stories – especially those involving his war wound. Typical of his cheerful personality was leaving the Senior Common Room £250 in order that its members could have a drink on him after his death. He died suddenly of a massive heart attack on 19 November 1992. On the following 15 February the University honoured him with an ecumenical service attended by about two hundred people.

Andrew is survived by two daughters, two grandchildren and five great grandchildren.

18

Patrick Brendan Kennedy 1929–66

Siobhán Vernon
University College Cork

I T GIVES ME GREAT pleasure to write a short account of the life of Patrick Brendan Kennedy, known affectionately as Paddy or PBK. He was Professor of Mathematics in University College, Cork (UCC) from 1956 to 1963, and Professor of Mathematics in the University of York from 1963 until his tragic death in 1966, just one month before his 37th birthday.

His academic career was very impressive:

1946   Leaving Certificate Examination: first place in Ireland in Irish composition, 98 per cent in Mathematics, honours in all subjects. Awarded the Honan and College Entrance Scholarships to UCC.[1] Came to UCC intending to study Medicine, but was dissuaded from doing so by the then President,[2] who interviewed all incoming students. Opted for a BSc in Mathematics and Mathematical Physics.

1949   First Class Honours BSc

1949–51   Demonstrator in the Mathematics and Mathematical Physics Departments. Duties were to lecture, and assist in setting and

---

[1] He was very disciplined and told me that during a heatwave he studied in a cold bath.

[2] Alfred O'Rahilly, MA PhD DLitt DSc, a man of 'apparent multidisciplinary omniscience' (John A. Murphy, *The College – A History of Queen's / University College, Cork*).

marking examination papers.

1951   First Class Honours MSc, Travelling Studentship of the National University of Ireland (NUI).

1951–53   Research Assistant in the University College of the South West (now the University of Exeter) under Walter Hayman.[3]

1953–54   Assistant Lecturer in Mathematics, Aberystwyth.

1954   PhD (NUI), the title of his thesis being 'On the Growth of Certain Integral and Subharmonic Functions'. In this year he married Pamela Fishwick in Aberystwyth.

1954–56   Lecturer in Mathematics, UCC.

1956–63   Professor of Mathematics, UCC.

1960   DSc (NUI).

1961   Elected Member of the Royal Irish Academy.

1963–66   Professor of Mathematics, University of York.

Paddy's father and mother came from Kerry. His father first trained as a carpenter and later joined the Gárda Siochána. They had five children, Tadhg, Nancy,[4] Paddy, Kitty and Siobhán. They were a close-knit family and when appointed demonstrator in 1949 (at £300 p.a.), Paddy helped his brother Tadhg through college. Of the next generation, Paddy's children – Ann, David and Jane – became respectively a partner in charge of corporate finance for Deloitte and Touche for Southern England, Chief Executive for Gedling Borough Council, Nottingham and Operations Manager for the Safer York Partnership (or York's Crime-buster as Jane was described in a recent newspaper article). Two mathematicians appeared in Tadhg's family – his sons Colm (Professor of Statistics in Purdue University), and Mel (Lecturer in Computer Studies in University College Dublin).

Paddy was a man of many parts – a complex and sometimes contradictory personality – considered difficult by some, but never dull. He could be charming or distant, witty or 'not amused', extravert or introvert, tolerant or intolerant, easy-going or intimidating, kind or sarcastic, laid back or perfectionist. But in one thing he was consistent and uncompromising – his sense of justice and fair play. He was very

---

[3]   Professor W.K. Hayman, FRS, now Senior Research Fellow and Emeritus Professor of Mathematics, Imperial College, London.

[4]   Nancy treasures a memory of little brother PBK aged 2 or 3 running out of their back door with dinner leftovers for a neighbour's chickens; his reward was a drop of stout.

patriotic – at least one hotel register bore the entry, NATIONALITY: 'Irish, thank God' after his name – and had a deep love of the Irish language.

A wonderful teacher with an ability to think on his feet, Paddy was quite happy to walk to and fro in front of an honours class while silently teasing out some idea or alternative viewpoint that had just occurred to him. His early lecture notes were clear and flawless, handwritten in a copperplate script; later notes were equally clear and flawless but type-written. He had marvellous clarity and an ability to communicate his enthusiasm and insight. Paddy inspired great loyalty in his students, a loyalty that is still evident today, more than thirty years after his death. Many distinguished past pupils of his testify to his teaching abilities. Michael Mortell, President of UCC from 1989 to 1999, wrote: 'Paddy Kennedy was the best lecturer I ever had. He made a profound impression on me by his crystal clear, beautifully paced lectures. Despite his somewhat stern exterior, as a young student beginning Mathematics, I found him very sympathetic.The present President, Gerard T. Wrixon, as a Third Electrical Engineering Student in 1960, was taught by Paddy and remembers him as 'a superb and lucid teacher' whose lectures were 'precise and insightful'. Interestingly he says that PBK was the first person he ever heard use the word 'black box' now commonly used in engineering jargon. Paddy Barry[5] describes him as a watershed in the department. Finbarr Holland[6] remembers him 'as a teacher of a subject that he clearly loved, who possessed to the nth degree an economy of style and elegance of presentation that would be hard to match whether orally or in writing.' Another former student, D. Ó Mathúna, described Paddy as a lifesaver to them when he returned to Cork in 1954.[7] Brian Twomey[8] speaks of his charisma. Until you came to know him, he could, however, appear intimidating. Once, during a lecture, he offered cigarettes to the class saying 'Have one'. One of the students had never smoked before, but was afraid to decline. He lit up, coughed and spluttered and nearly choked to death much to the amusement of the others.

His colleagues too have wonderful memories of Paddy. Vincent Hart[9] talks movingly about PBK's personal impact, his marvellous companion-

[5] Professor P.D. Barry, PBK's successor as head of the Mathematics Department.
[6] Professor F. Holland, UCC.
[7] D. Ó Mathuna was, later, a Travelling Studentship winner. He felt that the senior lecturers in the department, who were applying for higher offices, did not have sufficient time for the students.
[8] Professor B. Twomey, UCC.
[9] Dr V. Hart was lecturer in the Mathematical Physics Department, and later emigrated to Australia.

ship, his wit, his instinct for quality in whatever interested him, whether music (classical and traditional Irish), poetry, or cigarettes (although his enthusiasm for Turkish cigarettes engendered some pungent comments in the staff common room). One of the very few things that did not engage his interest was sport. Vincent, too, remembers him as a superbly clear lecturer and a first class research mathematician, while W.H. McCrea[10] wrote to Vincent that 'PBK going so young was the great tragedy of the Irish mathematical scene'. As a former student and colleague of Paddy's, I owe him a tremendous debt. He took a personal interest in my career and, apart from my family, was by far the most significant influence on my life. As godmother to his son David I was made to feel part of his extended family. Inadvertently, he was responsible for my becoming a non-smoker; as a young staff member, I smoked only occasionally, but found that when proffering cigarettes Paddy would not take no for an answer. I realised that the only way I could be in control was to stop smoking. He accepted then that I did not smoke, but curiously would not accept that I did not drink and regularly pressurised me in that respect.

Research held a very high priority for Paddy Kennedy. His research career began in 1951 when he joined Walter Hayman, then lecturer in Exeter, as his first research student. Hayman writes nostalgically; 'The following two years were very happy for us both. We were young and enthusiastic and had long conversations about functions walking in Rougement gardens and other places around Exeter. . . . Paddy was a wonderful conversationalist and tremendous good company. I have known few greater joys in life than sitting opposite him each smoking a cigarette and chatting, oblivious of time'.[11] In his article on Paddy Kennedy, Hayman gives a very comprehensive account of Kennedy's research which dealt primarily with asymptotics. He worked mainly in three fields: functions of a complex variable, Fourier series with gaps and Tauberian theorems. He published twenty papers in eleven years and was also writing a book on applications of subharmonic functions to function theory. Unfinished at the time of his death, this was subsequently finished and published, under their joint names, by Professor Hayman.[12] Hayman included the tribute 'to a deeply conscientious and

---

[10] Sir W.H. McCrea, who was Professor of Mathematics in Royal Holloway College, London, when Paddy spent a year there on sabbatical leave.

[11] W.K. Hayman, 'Patrick Brendan Kennedy', *Journal of the London Mathematical Society*, **42**, 1967, p. 559.

[12] W.K. Hayman and P.B. Kennedy, (1996) *Subharmonic Functions*, Vol. 1, London: Academic Press.

extremely charming person whom I still miss greatly'. He considered Paddy to be one of Britain's most able function theorists.

PBK was very generous with his ideas and with his time. I have particularly fond memories of doing research with him in my office one glorious summer in 1964, when he was on holidays with his family in Cork – it may have been a busman's holiday for him, but he seemed to enjoy it as much as I did. My recollection is that he treated me as an equal, which was wonderful for one who felt very unequal indeed. Sadly my diffidence led to a misunderstanding between us sometime later when I was no longer his research student. He asked me whether I would be interested in doing a joint paper. There was nothing I would have liked better, but I demurred feeling sure he would be bound to contribute the lion's share, which I thought would be unfair to him. Unfortunately he must have thought I was unappreciative and became annoyed. I was too shocked to try to retrieve the situation, something I have regretted ever since. It was one of the few times he revealed to me the insecurities that apparently dogged his life.

At UCC he espoused the cause of anyone he felt was treated unfairly by the administration. He had experienced discrimination himself. In 1953, the post of combined lecturer in Mathematics and Mathematical Physics was created with a certain person in mind. This man and Paddy applied and each was required to sit an examination in Irish, as it was a prerequisite that a successful candidate be able to lecture through Irish. Paddy passed the test and the favourite son did not. The post was abolished, PBK returned to Exeter and the other candidate obtained a lectureship in another department. At that time there were no Boards of Assessors in the National University of Ireland to advise on appointments, but there was a curious regulation: 'Canvassing is forbidden but candidates may interview governors'. Canvassing, however, was widespread and abuse of the system was not uncommon. One voter did not even know the correct name of the candidate he had promised to vote for.[13] This was anathema to PBK.

Paddy was appointed lecturer in Mathematics in Cork in 1954, and applied in 1955 for the Chair, which became vacant when his predecessor was made President of UCC. No appointment was made and the post was re-advertised. Paddy knew that an effort had been made to block him. One colleague argued, in good faith I would think, that 'if we

[13] See Murphy, *The College*, p. 322, for the story of the voter who was looking for Lucy (male surname) when he should have been looking for Lucy (female first name).

don't appoint Kennedy we will have two good men in the department; if we do, we will only have one'. However, this time his qualifications were awarded their due merit: he was appointed Professor.[14] Enthusiastically he set to work, with no office (his predecessor being Registrar, had an office *ex-officio*), and hence no telephone; he had no secretary – just access to a typing pool. By 1959 he had acquired an office; a telephone followed, but he never had the luxury of a departmental secretary while in Cork.

Paddy was a devoted husband and father. Although he could bury himself in his work, it meant a great deal to him that his family was there for him when he surfaced. On one occasion, when flying out from Dublin together to a mathematical colloquium in England, Paddy and I had hurriedly to take a taxi to the airport, as he had spent so long in town selecting a present for his wife Pam. She wrote that he adored his children, and I can recall how proudly he detailed their exploits. He and Pam were extremely convivial, and loved to entertain. Paddy did not mind if it was just drinks or a formal dinner party, as long as there were people. I can remember him commenting on a friend and colleague who entertained lavishly, but rarely; PBK would have preferred little and often. The social life of UCC and especially of the Mathematics Department was enriched by the presence of Paddy and Pam and they regularly formed most enjoyable parties to dinner-dances. In College, Paddy's office was a social centre where friends were welcome to drop in for coffee.

Alfie Madden[15] reminded me of Paddy's interest in the Cork Mathematics Teachers Association. At one of their meetings, Paddy explained his ideas for the setting of scholarship papers. Present at the talk was a former student of his who objected to having logarithms on such a paper on the grounds that they required only memory work. PBK set him up, rather cruelly in my opinion. He put a logarithmic equality on the board and asked 'would you call that memory work?' When the man replied in the affirmative Paddy retorted 'then your memory must be damn bad – that minus should be a plus'.

An excellent correspondent, he wrote to me until the year of his death. His letters were light-hearted, mostly about mathematics and family matters, and usually very witty. In one he discussed 'good', 'very good', and 'bad' sequences and added 'Thus you may keep the high moral tone by considering good (and very good) sequences only'. Having defined

[14] UC Record 1957, UCC archives.
[15] Retired secondary schoolteacher and part-time lecturer in the Mathematics Department, UCC.

'φ-good sequences', he allows himself a pun: 'As Shakespeare says, 'φ upon it! Ah, φ!' He then defines ψ-good sequences and puns again: 'I leave it at this. No doubt you will heave a ψ of relief'. This letter was written on 20 April 1966, just seven weeks before his death. At the time he was dealing with, and worrying about, the first set of degree examinations in York as well as examinations in the National University of Ireland where he had accepted the job of external examiner. In fact he wrote 'I am writing at home, at the mid-hour of night, having decided to relax from exam-papers (NUI and York) by writing to you' – and in a footnote 'Re-reading: have I paid you a compliment or the opposite?'

Paddy was a perfectionist in almost everything he undertook. Pam writes that he was never satisfied with his work and was always striving for perfection; even when composing limericks for his family and friends, he always insisted on correct grammar. He studied the piano in his senior years in the Christian Brothers secondary school (the North Monastery) and, later, under Frau Tilly Fleischmann, whose son was Professor of Music in UCC. Frau Fleischmann said of him at the time that he was the only pupil she had had who never played a wrong note. Through his interest in the piano he became very friendly with the musician Seán Ó Riada, later internationally renowned; they played the piano, smoked and drank together as students. I think that he must have discontinued the piano, however, as neither Vincent Hart nor I was aware that he could play. He was also an excellent chess player and was largely instrumental in revivifying the Chess Club in College[16] while a student. He became Irish Chess Champion in 1949. As was the case with the piano he then seemed to lose interest. When appointed Professor of Mathematics in 1956, he immediately set about raising standards and building up the department, which was vigorous and thriving when he resigned in 1963 to go to York. The President of the College (his predecessor in the chair of Mathematics) with whom he had had many clashes, generously wrote to him at the time 'I have always admired the excellent manner in which you ran the Department and its vitality in the domain of teaching and research'.[17] During his seven years as Professor, four of his students were awarded the Travelling Studentship in Mathematical Science.

Tributes paid to him in Cork were mirrored by those of his colleagues

[16]   His friends Jack Casey (now an African Mission priest in Nigeria) and Ferdie O'Halloran (retired lecturer in Civil Engineering, UCC) have fond memories of shared matches and subsequent long walks from house to house.

[17]   I note from the UCC archives that the President later wrote and asked Paddy if he would consider withdrawing his resignation.

Patrick Brendan Kennedy

Maurice Dodson and Arnold Arthurs[18] in York, who kindly sent me their recollections of Paddy. They, too, talked of his humour, his warmth and kindness, his informality and great gift of friendship – his friends' problems became his problems. Concerned that Arthurs had six unbroken years of teaching, he encouraged him to spend a year in America on sabbatical and arranged for his leave from York. The night before the flight Paddy and one or two colleagues called and a rather hectic social evening ensued. This was in September 1965 and Paddy died before the sabbatical year was over. In York, Paddy's genius and formidable mathematical power were evident, and mathematicians came to York because of his distinction. He carried the high standards and scrupulous attention to detail, which characterised his mathematics, over into his administration and running of the department. He had 'the grand vision' and his staff were glad to help with the details of putting it into effect. He took teaching very seriously and used homely analogies to put his ideas across. His deep love of analysis led him to teach it with 'passion and commitment' although he was always conscious of the needs of the weaker students. He mixed business with pleasure, however. As was in the case in Cork, his office was an extension of the coffee room and there many mathematical and educational points were discussed, enlivened by his endless fund of anecdotes.

Paddy's working habits must have put a great strain on him. His sister Nancy recalls that, as a college student, he would study continuously for 24 hours and then more or less pass out. It would be impossible to waken him. His wife, Pam wrote that, of the professors appointed to new departments in English universities in 1963, he was the only one who did not have a year free to spend on preparing for the inauguration. He had to continue with his work in Cork while also establishing a departmental library in York, interviewing candidates for academic posts there, arranging courses and interviewing prospective students. In the midst of all of this, he had by then accepted that he had a problem with alcoholism, although for the last year of his life he was a teetotaller. With hindsight it is clear he had had much to cope with. He suffered from depression and was receiving treatment. He had left friends in Cork, and moved into a new environment. On the other hand, in February 1964, he wrote to his friend Seán Teegan[19] that 'Life is enjoyable here, in a hard working – occasionally very! – sort of way . . . . I am blessed with a very bright

[18] Dr M. Dodson and Professor A. Arthurs were appointed lecturers in York in 1964 and 1963 respectively.

[19] Professor S. Teegan, Emeritus Professor of Chemistry, UCC.

nucleus of staff . . . and the powers-that-be are pretty reasonable . . . It makes me a wee bit sad, now and then, that I have not had one single moment of regret for UCC (other than regret at leaving a few friends).'

Professor Hayman wrote that Paddy achieved much but at high cost to his nerves. 'He was extremely conscientious and his final breakdown can only be attributed to excessive and quite unnecessary worry about his students and his work'.[20] This breakdown tragically culminated in his death by his own hand in 1966. His colleagues in York and in Cork were deeply shocked. The P. B. Kennedy Prize for the best finals student was instituted by the department in York as a well-deserved tribute to the part Paddy played in the foundation of their very successful degree.

We lost a warm-hearted and sympathetic friend. Writing this article has been a very emotional experience for me: it was a privilege to have known him.

Slán leat a Phádraig, ar lámh dheis Dé go raibh d'anam.

Bibliography

W.K. Hayman (1967) 'Patrick Brendan Kennedy', *Journal of the London Mathematical Society*, **42**, 559–68.

W.K. Hayman and P.B. Kennedy (1976) *Subharmonic Functions*, Vol. 1, London: Academic Press.

John A. Murphy (1995) *The College – A History of Queen's / University College, Cork*. Cork: Cork University Press.

---

[20] Hayman, 'Patrick Brendan Kennedy', p. 560.